Father and
Retired

*The Life Stories of
Quintin Ramil, Sr. & Jr.*

By Quintin R. Ramil, Jr.

To Pepe & Margre,

Long time friends —

Published by Asian Journal San Diego
The original and first Asian Journal in America
E-Mail: asianjournal@aol.com

Dedication

Father and Son, USN Retired is dedicated to my wife, Teresita, who stood behind me during this writing.

To my children, Ram, Ray, Tressy and Roxanne who encouraged me to write my family's story.

To my grandchildren, Reilly Jane Kopka, Shane Reese Ramil, Madeline Page Snowdon, Raegan Terese Kopka, Reece James Ramil Kopka, Elizabeth Quinn Snowdon and Michael Ramil Snowdon so that they may know where their grandfather came from.

Books published by
Asian Journal San Diego:

Promised Land by Simeon G. Silverio Jr.

Betel Nuts and Other Stories by Simeon G. Silverio, Jr.

Philippine Homecoming's Cherished Memories – by Simeon G. Silverio, Jr.

Complicated Affairs by Simeon G. Silverio, Jr.

The Boys of Summer and Other Stories by Simeon G. Silverio, Jr.

Balik Tanaw – The Lives and Loves of Filipino Movie Stars of Yesteryears by Dr. Romy Protacio

Isang Laksang Tula ng mga Piling Katatawanan ni Joe Cabrera

Rice Cooker: Writings on Filipino Americal Life, Issues and People by Simeon G. Silverio Jr.

The Life and Times of a Filipino-American In San Diego, California by Simeon G. Silverio Jr

Philippine Visit's Precious Memories by Simeon G. Silverio, Jr.

Philippine Travels' Treasured Memories by Simeon G. Silverio, Jr.

The Rain In Spain and Other Travel Stories by Simeon G. Silverio, Jr.

To order a copy, send $12.95 ($595 Philippine Pesos) plus $3.00 ($138 Philippine Pesos) to **Asian Journal San Diego**, 550 East 8th Street, Suite 6, National City, CA 91950 or MEG Silverio Press, 432 Platerias, Quiapo, Manila. For more information, e-mail sandiegoasianjournal@yahoo.com or call (619) 474-0588 (U.S.A) or 7335455 (Philippines)

Acknowledgments

I want to acknowledge my family and friends, especially my nieces who kept asking me how we are related to each other.

To my friends Mario and Purita Firme, Janet and Lillian, who were stranded with Tere and me on one of the Caramoan Islands off Naga, Camarines Sur, Philippines. Because of the weather condition, we could not visit the other islands and were advised to just stay put. We spent many hours just telling stories. I told them the story of my father, fathering a child during the war and they encouraged me to write a story about it.

To my co-Senior Mentor for San Diego County, Ms. Vikky Anders, who encouraged me and gave me pointers on how to make it an interesting book.

To my Inay (mother in Filipino) who always kept a journal and is really the writer in our family.

About the Author

Quintin R. Ramil, Jr. retired from the U.S. Navy as a Chief Legalman. He was formerly a Chief Radioman having served on board several submarines and was a Navy Instructor.

He attended Manila Central University, Manila Law College and Palomar College and holds a certificate as a Registered Certified Financial Advisor (RCFA) from Clayton University. He is a proud father of four children. Quintin, III and Ramon graduated from the U.S. Naval Academy, class of '86 and '88 respectively. Tressy graduated from California State University, Long Beach with a degree in Education and Roxanne graduated from California State University, Sacramento with a degree in Communication Studies.

Quint's in depth training includes special real estate courses such as Floyd Wickman's Sweathogs, Real Estate Practice, Economics, Financing, Property Management, Legal Practice, Real Estate Investments and Creative Financing. He was the founder and Charter President of the U.S. Naval Academy Parents Club of San Diego and the Fil-Am Toastmasters Club of San Diego No. 9493. He holds the title of Advanced Communicator (Gold) and Community Leader.

Quint and his wife of more than 50 years, Teresita Roxas Ramil, are active in Airman's Chapel Marine Corps Air Station Miramar as choir members, Reader and Eucharistic Minister respectively. He enjoys group singing, golf, gardening, grandparenting to their seven grandchildren, dancing and traveling all over the world. And he also loves to tell jokes.

Table of Contents

Introduction

Stories – the true ones – are interesting in how they develop. Some stories are buried and forgotten, some are put away for years and slowly surface and some are gathered and released in a book because someone said that was the thing to do. Such is the case with this book. People said it was time, and more importantly, that it needed to be done.

Of course with a book, an honest book, skeletons are undoubtedly going to come out of the closet. For instance, recently while I was stranded with some friends on an island off Naga, province of Camarines Sur, Philippines, I told them the story of my dad fathering a child out of wedlock during the war, and they all implied there may be other stories there as well.

So I tried to start this, but for some reason I kept postponing. Maybe some of those skeletons weren't ready to come out yet. Who knows? But one day opportunity presented itself. I had to get some things done in the Philippines by myself, and I found the time to do it. I had no more excuses.

This is the result of that very focused time, encompassing more than seventy-four years. This includes time from my father and his stories, and my stories, all wrapped up in family. I was the only one of seven children who followed my father's footsteps, which included time on board U.S. Navy ships. Please understand this is not a sailor's diary. This is a glimpse behind the scenes of a family, friends, and neighbors who in ways both large and small, shaped part of the world in which we live in. Some names have been intentionaly changed to protect the innocent.

Prologue

Every family has its members and friends; those who help create the story. These are some of mine...

My grandfather, Emeterio Ramil, was born in the barrio of Carinio, town of Paniqui, Province of Tarlac in the Philippines. He was married to Maria Apuan, from the town of Anao, Tarlac, and they had six children. The oldest a daughter, Valentina, was married to Pablo Yanos whose ancestors were from Bacarra, Ilocos Norte as were the Ramils. The second child, a son named, Lope, settled in the town of Cuyapo, province of Nueva Ecija, after marrying Imen Reginaldo. The third child, a son Pedro, became a minister of the IEMILIF (Iglesia Evangelica Metodista Inlas Islas Filipinas) church, a local version of the Methodist church, and married Maria Bernardino from the town of Novaliches, City of Caloocan, in the province of Rizal. He was assigned as a pastor in the town. The fourth child, Quintin, was named after his uncle, Quintin Apuan, locally known as "Pop" by the Americans as he had a fatherly look and owned a bar in Pasay, a city in the outskirts of Manila. The fifth, a daughter, Rosalia, never married and was active as a deaconess in the Methodist church in the town of Paniqui, Tarlac. The sixth, a daughter named Consolacion, was a nurse who graduated from Mary Johnston hospital in the town of Tondo, city of Manila. She encouraged my mother to give birth at Mary Johnston hospital. She served in the Philippine Army Nurse Corps during the war.

Living on a farm, Quintin helped his father tend to the animals. His primary duties were to make sure that their carabaos or water buffalos were taken to the river at least once a day where they would drink, wade, and swim and were given a scrubbing. The family raised rice and a variety of vegetables like tomatoes, squash, bitter melons, eggplants and many more. They also had several coconut trees. I still remember our grandfather bringing all these goodies to our home in Novaliches in the 1950's.

Once while Quintin was herding his team of carabaos, he found himself in the middle of a swollen river. The animals were having a difficult time crossing and were actually being swept by the strong current. He almost drowned but managed to keep the animals together and successfully crossed the river.

After graduating from high school, he was informed by his older brother, Pedro, that a new dam will be constructed in Novaliches. They were hiring anyone old enough but they will be required to have their own carabao and cart and of course a shovel and a pick. He did not waste any time. He borrowed a cart from his oldest brother, Lope, and with one of the family carabaos he gathered his menial belongings and proceeded to travel from Carinio to Novaliches, a surburb in the City of Caloocan. He travelled during the day and camped out by the roadside at night. I am still amazed as to how he managed to reach Novaliches which was about 120 kilometers away. It took him more than a month before he reached Novaliches. He stayed with his brother while working at what is now known as La Mesa Dam Eco Park.

It was at this time when he met Fausta M. Reyes, a seamstress working at a haberdashery store owned by a Mr. Zacarias Biglang-awa, a relative. Fausta is the daughter of Reverend Arcadio Reyes, also a minister of the Philippine version of the Methodist church and was also assigned in

Novaliches as co-pastor of Pedro Ramil. Quintin meets the daughter of the co-pastor of his brother. She was only 17 years old. He sees her almost every Sunday in church. It is very common for the pastors and their family to have lunch together after the service and that was the opportunity for him to get to know her better. Arcadio was single when he married Gregoria Matos, a widow with two young children. The oldest, a daughter named Onang and a son Martin. Onang lived with her family in the town of Marikina and was always a welcome sight when she visits our family. She would always have goodies for us. Arcadio and Gregoria had three children of their own. The oldest, a girl they named Fausta. The second and third both boys were named Mateo or Tayong and Canuto or Otong respectively. Canuto died at an early age. He was walking in a rice field when a deadly snake struck him. This was very common in the Philippines. He left a wife, Maxima Franco Reyes, and two children, a son named Ruben, and a daughter, Gloria. Mateo married Ciriaca Bernabe from a nearby barrio and their marriage was blessed with eight children. The oldest, a son, was named Alfredo or Eddie who was only a few months older than me. The second, another son, was named Ernesto or P I. The third, a son named Reynaldo or Small as he looked like our grandfather. The fourth a daughter was named Teresita and is married to Dr. Gerry Canlas and now lives in Orlando, Florida. The fifth is Romulo who stayed with us when I was stationed at Naval Communication Station Philippines and he was also able to visit us in San Diego. The sixth is Arcadio or Archie who went to dental school but did not practice as he went abroad and settled in San Jose, California with his family. The seventh is Carlos who still lives in Novaliches with his family. The youngest is Fernando. He owns several businesses and lives in Lipa City, Batangas. I have visited his three farms where he breeds fighting cocks, dogs and racing horses. He owns a funeral home in the city of Lipa, province of Batangas.

Chapter 1

Enlisting in the U.S. Navy

Working under the hot summer sun for days and days, digging and shoveling dirt was so back breaking. He did this for more than two years. The only thing he could look forward to was on Sundays when he would attend the service at his brother's church. On many occasions he would join the family for lunch. It was in one these occasions when he was introduced to the oldest daughter of the other pastor, Fausta Reyes.

Quintin decided to go to the city to find a better job. He takes his carabao and cart and proceeded to Manila and temporarily finds a job as an all around helper in a Catholic church in the City of Malate, a surburb of Manila. His many duties included cleaning the church and the facilities. On Sundays he would also assist as an altar boy for the masses. Then he heard that the US Navy was recruiting Filipinos. He tried to get information from anyone. He knew that there would be an examination so he began studying and did a lot of praying. He was lucky enough to pass the exam. This was to be the turning point in his life. The dream of many young Filipinos is to be able to go to America. In his joy and excitement he went to Luneta, a park in the City of Manila, and let his aging carabao loose as he knew he would soon board a transport ship that will take him and his fellow recruits to America. Today there is a monument in Luneta which could be a tribute to the carabao found roaming freely in that park many years ago.

Quintin was sworn into the US Navy in July 1929. He took his training in Great Lakes, Illinois. It was here that he became involved with an American woman. It was unclear where she lived but he fathered a son and they named him Carlos Ramil.

While stationed aboard several ships in the Pacific fleet, my dad was a boxer in the Navy and was at one time the All Navy champion in the 118 pound division. One of his teammates was Federico Ramirez, whose family also lived in Novaliches and has a son named Rico. We met for the first time in 1948 when their family returned to the Philippines from Rhode Island and stopped by to visit us in Hawaii. Today Fred lives with his family in Suisun, California. He is a retired Master Sergeant from the U.S. Air Force.

As a Navy man my dad fulfilled what was expected of him by his parents. This has been a tradition that is still going on today. Parents expect their children to provide for them. The goal of most Filipinos is to finish school so he or she can help their parents provide for the rest of the siblings. Early on my father established a scholarship for his younger sister and his oldest niece. He helped Consolacion and Maria Ramil Yanos finish their studies. These two ladies became nurses and in turn helped their own families. I remember my Manang (older relative) Mareng providing financial assistance for her siblings even after she had her own family. This is a very noble tradition common to many Filipino families. He continued to write Fausta and they were exchanging letters every week.

After four years in the US Navy, my dad returned to the Philippines to marry the woman who would become our mother, Fausta M. Reyes. I believe that at one time, my mother told me that they were engaged for almost six years.

The marriage took place in Novaliches on December 2, 1934. Looking at their wedding picture, I noticed that one of the bridesmaids was Tia Acang the wife of Uncle Mateo, and one of the sponsors was Faustino Reyes, a brother of my grandfather. Lolo Tino as we knew him was one of the first Filipinos recruited by the American Pineapple company to work as a laborer in Hawaii. He was recruited in 1928. It was my father who met him in Hawaii and advised him to return to the Philippines before the war broke out. He returned and was able to buy land in the outskirts of Novaliches. Dad continued to be stationed aboard many ships in the Pacific Fleet including one that was part of the Great White Fleet that sailed around the world.

After four years my mother gave birth to her first child. I was born on April 12, 1938. To my surprise, when I obtained a copy of my birth certificate from Mary Johnston Hospital in 1956, my birth date was recorded as April 11. It was obvious that the nurse who entered the date came to work on April 11 but I was born 10 minutes after midnight on the night of April 11 and so for 17 years I celebrated my birthday on the 12th. Today I do the only sensible thing and celebrate it on both days.

Sometime in 1941 my dad received orders to the USS Chaumont, a submarine tender home ported in Sangley Point Naval Base, Cavite, Philippines. My parents rented an apartment in Ermita, Manila close to the highway that goes to Cavite and he would commute from Ermita to Sangley Point navy base by bus.

In November of 1941, the USS Sargo, a submarine, tied up to the USS Chaumont, a submarine tender, needing a steward and was asking for volunteers. My dad volunteered and became a crewmember of the USS Sargo (SS-188).

In early December the USS Sargo was ordered to hold an open house in Manila Bay, which was very close to his apartment in Ermita, a surburb of the city of Manila. He was off that week-end but returned to his submarine to pick up his pay check. He planned to take me with him but my mom said that she was going to give me a bath and that was the only reason I stayed behind. When my dad arrived at his ship, he was barely on board when Japanese planes began bombing the City of Manila. This was December 8, 1941 the very same time Pearl Harbor was being attacked. As the USS Sargo was backing away from the pier, it was hit by a torpedo fired by one of the fighter planes. The Sargo lost one of its propellers. The crew could not help but see the devastation Manila suffered. My dad saw the whole city burning. He honestly believed that he lost his family. With one propeller, the Sargo still managed to reach Australia where my dad again volunteered for another submarine to go on a patrol. It was his compadre, Brigido Tamayo, my God father, who advised him to rest for a while and not go on another patrol just yet. This is what saved him as the submarine he was to board did not return and was listed as lost at sea. At this time he was due for rotation and received orders for Panama where he was to become the commissary store officer. He was promoted to Chief.

As a commissary store officer he was in charge of a big grocery store where many Panamanian women worked. It was there he met Inah, one of the store's cashiers. Believing that he no longer had a family, he and Inah lived together and became lovers. In 1942 Inah gave birth to a daughter and they named her Gwen. The three of them lived together as a family and he loved his daughter very much. He told me that Gwen would run after him when he left for work and always ran to greet him when he returned. Unknown to

18

him, he also had a daughter, Norma, who was born during the war. When he left Panama, he asked one of his men, petty officer Manuel Archuleta to look after his loved ones for him. As his chief, Mr. Archuleta had a very good relationship with my father and considered him as his idol and mentor. He not only took care of Inah, he married her and adopted her daughter. They did not have any children of their own. Eventually, they settled in San Diego, California. Gwen grew up not knowing any other father except for Mr. Archuleta.

Chapter 2

Life During the War

The people of the City of Manila were in panic. Bombs were exploding, buildings were burning, and the sounds of sirens were everywhere. The whole population must have been on the move as all modes of transportation were packed with people. I still do not know how my grandfather, the Reverend Arcadio Reyes, managed to get to the city from our town of Novaliches, a distance of about 30 miles in order to help his daughter and grandson evacuate. We were walking and running and trying to get a ride to the countryside. With one suitcase in hand and me perched on his shoulders, my grandfather just kept on walking with my mom close behind carrying some bags of whatever she could take with her. We managed to get to the city known as Blumentritt. This is where the busses bound for our town of Novaliches begin their route. Looking back and placing myself in my grandfather's shoes, I cannot imagine what a father would do when he heard that the city where his only daughter and grandson was living was being bombed and the whole city was burning. He took the first bus he could to go to Manila and just ran towards Ermita. My grandfather and mother walked from Ermita to Blumentritt a distance of about ten miles.

No bus would stop for anyone except when specifically given orders by someone in a position to do so. That was my Uncle Canuto. He was a Halili Bus Inspector and well liked by his drivers. He gave specific instructions to any drivers who happen to see his father and sister to pick them up. Before long a bus full of people stopped for us.

We arrived in Novaliches where we owned a big house just off the main road. It was a two story home with the main floor portion converted into a sari-sari store. Sari-sari means variety; a small convenience store. There was a Japanese fellow, married to a Filipina that used to deliver goods to my mom's store. He lived in the area and was known by the community. He in turn knew about everyone else, and this was the problem. He knew that my dad was a member of the US Navy. As soon as the Japanese forces landed, "Apa" as he was popularly known also donned his Japanese Army uniform. He was with the intelligence unit of the Japanese Imperial Army. The first group of Japanese soldiers to land was the Korean detachment. They were the meanest bunch of soldiers in the world and they proved it. This was the group that killed babies by tossing them in the air and spearing them with their bayonets. They raped women as they made their way around the countryside. Thanks to Apa, our family name, Ramil, was instantly on their wanted list, because we were related to a member of the United States military.

Many of our neighbors and townmates were leaving our town and so our family also began making preparations. My mom was pregnant so we had to wait until she gave birth to my sister, Norma, who was named after a movie actress, Norma Blancaflor. She was born on July 10, 1942. Soon my grandfather decided that we all join his brother, Faustino, who recently returned from Hawaii and was able to buy a farm in the outskirts of Novaliches known as "Pasong Putik". It was my father who ran into him in Honolulu just before the war and suggested that he return to the Philippines. He had a house big enough for two families and about an acre of land

22

to plant vegetables. There was also a river and a creek nearby loaded with fish, shrimp and fresh water clams.

My cousins and I were oblivious of the world's situation. We were happy doing what was expected from us. The two families were my uncle Tayong and his family, my mother and my grandmother and grandfather, and our great uncle Lolo (grandpa) Tino. There were four of us kids, my two cousins Eddie and Ernesto, my sister, Norma and I. Eddie who was a few months older than me was almost five years old. He was my partner in doing our assigned chores. We always did things together as we were the oldest of the kids. Our duties were to fetch water from a well which was about three hundred yards from our house. It was located between the river and the creek. We also had to fish, hunt and gather fruits and firewood. We learned how to catch shrimps by making a hideout for them. We assembled and bundled twigs and tied them together. Then we lowered the trap in the deep part of the creek and left it there overnight. In the morning we would take a net and place it under the twigs. Shrimps would be jumping as we raised the net to the surface. We would gather them and take them home to be cooked by my aunt or my mother. Our grandfather also taught us how to build fish traps. We would dig out a small portion of the river bank, make a sort of a tunnel and build a fence to enclose the hollowed portion of the river bank. The fence was made of bamboos. The two middle pieces rest on a stick, which acted as the trigger. These two pieces of bamboo fence were heavier than the rest as it is packed with mud on top. When a fish enters the fenced in area it would touch the stick and will cause the weighted pieces to drop down. We caught a lot of fish this way.

We also raised a lot of plants like, yams, corn, rice and several varieties of vegetables. I can say one thing,

23

although many suffered hunger, our family was lucky enough to always have food for our existence. Our grandfather also taught us how to build animal traps. We caught quails, monitor lizards and even a young wild pig. We also became very good with our slingshots. I remember hitting a dove once while it was flying. We would also gather all kinds of fruits as the tropical climate was so conducive to local fruit trees and the abundance of papayas, star apples, jackfruits, santol and the ever available guavas made our life bearable. My favorite was gathering jicamas or singkamas in Tagalog. It grows all over and it was very easy to find. We would dig it from the ground using a pointed stick. This was our snack and it was so good. I particularly like the small ones for they were sweeter and much juicier than the big ones. There were a lot of yucca roots or what we call kamoteng kahoy. This was my second favorite. We would just pull the whole plant off the ground and we would place it on the bonfire. When the fire is out, our feast begins.

Oh and about Apa, the Japanese spy? We found out later on that a group of Filipino guerrillas were able to get hold of him after he donned his uniform and killed him. I believe that he did not have enough time to give his report to his superiors.

Our first order of business was to build an air raid shelter. We found the ideal location. Not far from our house were three mature santol trees. The trunks were about three feet in diameter (a local fruit that is sweet and sour and grows wild in our area) growing in a cluster but far enough from each other that we were able to dig out an air raid shelter between the three trees. Our two grandfathers and uncle Tayong took turns digging using a pick and a shovel. It took them almost a week to finally finish the digging and when it was finished it measured six feet by eight feet and about eight feet deep. We covered it over with bamboos, palm leaves and dirt. It had a built in steps so we can actually walk down into it. There was enough space for all of us, especially if we huddled. In one corner we stacked emergency supply of water in a big jug. We actually hid in the shelter whenever we hear unknown airplanes flying in the area. It also served as a very good hiding place when us kids played hide and seek.

On one occasion a platoon of Japanese soldiers got lost and ended up at our place. They decided to take a break and wanted to use our fire pit to cook their rice. Of course they did not have to ask for our permission. The problem was at about that time, a U.S. spotter plane was in the area and my grandfather was afraid that the pilot might just start shooting at the Japanese soldiers. So my grandfather literally pulled them and suggested they hide under the trees. He was ignored and they continued just sitting around in the open enjoying their lunch. It was a good thing that the spotter plane did not do anything else and continued its flight. This was a sign that big things were about to happen. Little did we know that General MacArthur was only a few days away from his promise to return.

We could sense that even the Japanese soldiers knew their days were getting short. They were no longer as mean as they used to be. At this time we made a plan to go to town to check out our house as we heard that it was occupied by a Japanese detachment and made into their headquarters. Because the civilians were no longer in great danger, my mom, auntie Acang, Eddie and I went down to the town. We arrived at our house and saw the damaged done by the soldiers that occupied it. It is now abandoned and run down. It was vandalized after the soldiers left. We saw some of what was left of our furnitures after using it as firewood.

Even parts of our house were burned. Garbage was strewn all around and the whole place was in disarray. We attempted to clean it as best we could and as we were rummaging through the kitchen cabinets, my aunt found some flour, which we managed to take back with us. When we arrived at the farm, my aunt did not waste any time. She started preparing dough from the flour she found and made some "butsi". This is like fritters made from flour dough and filled with sweetened yams and then deep fried. It is a very tasty and sought after delicacy. My cousin Eddie and I were down at the river checking on our traps so we were not around when the first batch of butsi were passed out to everyone. Our great uncle, Faustino, ate the most and all of a sudden his mouth began to froth and he went into convulsions. The others who had eaten the fritters also began experiencing food poisoning. This was the time everyone realized that the flour we found was not really flour but rat poison. Those who ate the butsi were given chunks of cubed brown cane sugar by my grandmother. This was a cure she learned early on. This is probably what saved us. Unfortunately, our granduncle, Faustino, was not able to recuperate. He died shortly, probably within two weeks. He was not able to see the Americans return. It just dawned on me that.....was my mother, Fausta, named after our great uncle? I should have known.

After several weeks and after our great uncle's funeral, my mom decided to return to our house. This we did. It took us again several days to make our house livable again. Lucky for us, our artesian well was still working. We had clean water and the pump was still functional. The storage tank on top of the roof was still in good condition. Our life was slowly turning normal. My uncle and his family lived across the street from us and they too were settled in. My grandfather and grandmother lived with us as our mother is their "Ine" or only daughter. One night, there was a big commotion and we heard gunshots. We were told to leave the area as the Americans had landed and a big fight with the Japanese soldiers would take place. We were to go to the next town. Everyone was on the move. Most of our relatives managed to stay together as we made our way to the next town. The road was packed with people. There was no way you could move about. You occupied your space and you just move forward in unison. We travelled all night and at daybreak we arrived at the next town called, Bagbag. Here we settled and rested our weary bodies just sitting by the side of the road. There were rice fields all around and we just laid there resting. We were told later on that behind us were the Japanese soldiers. They cleverly used us as their shield in the cover of the night. Once daylight came, they ran back into the woods. The Americans had not landed so it was a false alarm. We slowly returned to our houses, a distance of about ten miles. Not long afterwards we did see some American planes. They were firing at the fleeing Japanese soldiers.

Chapter 3

American Landing

All we heard were the roar and scrapping of tanks and bulldozers clearing the roadways. Before long a temporary bridge was built over the Tulyahan River that runs through our town. Then we saw a convoy of trucks (called 6x6) loaded with American soldiers. This was the first time for me to see an American. I could not figure out what they were chewing. I had never seen chewing gum before.

Then they set up camp in the town park; it comsisted of several tents complete with a dining hall and sleeping areas with portable cots. They also built portable showers and bathrooms. After every meal they would pass out their leftovers. There would be a line, mostly of kids including me, carrying one gallon cans and as we passed through, the cooks would scoop the leftovers into our cans. You never knew what you would get especially since we only had one can and they just filled it up with whatever. When I arrived home, my mom would sort it out. I remember getting some ham once. This was a jackpot for me. I became friends with many of the soldiers at that camp, but mostly with the cooks who I would try to impress by speaking some English words that my mom taught me. Mom also took in some laundry from the soldiers. She would accept their laundry and she would wash them in the river, dry them under the sun and then iron them. I remember a Mr. Remlo and a Mr. Kurtz as two of her customers. These two would look out for me when I got in line for leftovers. They would make sure I got some extras.

Soon the Americans left our town and a little bit of normalcy returned. I was soon enrolled in kindergarten. My grandparents still lived with us and we had not heard from our father. We checked with the Philippine National Red Cross and found out that he was alive. I always knew that we would see him again. It never crossed my mind that he could have gotten killed. Incidentally, the submarine that he was to go on patrol with from Australia did not return and was declared lost at sea. I guess my Godfather, Brigido Tamayo, who advised him not to volunteer, saved his life. I was told that during my baptismal, my Ninong (Godfather) brought with him his fiancé, Petronila Pimentel, from the city of Olongapo province of Zambales.

At this time my grandfather was assigned to a church in Banlat, a town nearby, as its pastor. On Sundays, he would take me with him. I remember that my mom would dress me up in a sailor suit and I knew some Tagalog poems which I would recite in front of the congregation before the start of the service. I would get standing ovations. After the service, we would be invited to various homes for lunch and I remember I would be given a special treat by our hosts. My grandfather was so proud of me.

During the week he would hunt and stuff animals, and birds like eagles and hawks, as he was a taxidermist on the side. He caught pythons, monitor lizards and big birds using different traps. He also collected butterflies and preserved them in picture frames. He would then peddle his goods to the different universities in Manila, selling to students and faculty. When he returned, he would always have goodies of us grandkids.

Philippine Liberation and the Return of My Father

My mom heard an announcement over the radio telling all US military dependents to report to the Philippine National Red Cross in Manila to be accounted for, so the three of us accompanied by my grandfather went to Manila to register. This is how my dad learned that we were alive. He immediately requested to be assigned to the Philippines and was lucky enough to be given orders to report to the Philippine Sea Frontier Command in Pasay, a surburb of Manila. It is very close to the waterfront and very far from Novaliches. My dad decided to purchase a house in Pasay. He found a new house next to his uncle, Quintin Apuan, who lived with his family at Libertad, Pasay. Our house was behind the City Pie Bakery on F.B. Harrison Street between Concepcion Street and Salud Street. It was just a few blocks from the base. My mom and my sister, Norma, joined him and lived there. I would continue living with my grandparents in Novaliches as I was already in school. I would join them on week-ends and I still managed to make many friends there. This was the time when we would play house and actually try to cook meals. Most of the time, I found myself just playing with my sister, Norma. I remember we were running in a circular motion and for some reason I turned and met her head on. We both suffered cuts and my scar is still visible today. I remember also that this was the very first time I was ever spanked by my father. I did not want to sleep alone in my bedroom and I insisted that I sleep next to them. I had to be spanked and I can honestly say that I learned a lesson because that was the first and only time I was ever spanked by my father.

Another incident that I will always remember is one weekend, my Godparents, Mr. And Mrs. Brigido Tamayo were visiting with their son, Brigido, Jr. I must have played very hard that day as they said I fell asleep earlier than normal and they all decided to go to the base for some ice cream. I was left behind with our maid as I was in a deep slumber. Later on when I woke up they were nowhere to be found. I went into a fit as I wanted so much to also eat ice cream at the base. That was the best part of visiting my parents on week-ends.

Some Sundays I would be with my grandfather in his new assignment as the new pastor of a church in the the town of Zapote, City of Bacoor Province of Cavite. It was the same routine. I would do some declamation and I would be given treats by members of the congregation. My grandfather was getting well known for having a grandson that recited poems before the service began.

Chapter 4

Leaving for Hawaii

After two years, my dad was once again due for transfer. He received orders to the Naval Air Station at Ford Island, Pearl Harbor, Hawaii. This time he had the option of taking his family with him. There are now three kids as my mother gave birth to a third child, a son, and he was named after our grandmother, Maria Apuan Ramil. Thus his name is Mario, who was born on June 21, 1946. Our family left for Hawaii in July of 1947 aboard the USNS Daniel I. Sultan, a MSTS (Military Ship Transportation Service) ship. We arrived in Hawaii after sailing the Pacific for 21 days. We lived in a converted quonset hut in a Navy housing for enlisted personnel and their families called Moanalua Navy Housing. It was next to the Navy Marine golf course not very far from the Naval Station Pearl Harbor. Norma and I enrolled at Pearl Harbor Kai Elementary School. I was in grade five and she was in grade one. My teacher was Mrs. Giddens. One of my classmates was the son of my father's ex shipmate, Pacifico Jose, Jr. They were from Cavite, Philippines. They lived next door to us and we both joined the Cub Scouts. Another neighbor who arrived later was my Godparents and their son Brigido, Jr., who became Junior No. 3. I was Junior No. 2 as Pacifico who came ahead of us was known as Junior No. 1 in the cub scouts.

Another family friend that also lived in the housing was Uncle Jose De Vega and Auntie Soccoro De Vega. They had a son, Joe and a daughter, Isa. Jose De Vega Jr., later on became an actor on Broadway and in the movies. He played the part of Chino in the movie West Side Story. Auntie Socco De Vega was friends with the Archuleta family as she and Inah came from the same town in Panama.

My father was going through the telephone white pages when he found the name of his uncle, Feliciano Apuan, a cousin of his mother, and lives in Kalihi, a town close to Honolulu, with his family. I remember meeting Auntie Orang, Uncle Johnny and Auntie Mary. I am still in touch with Auntie Mary today as she lives with her husband in Anaheim. Auntie Mary and her husband, John Buntrock, were able to attend our 50th wedding anniversary celebration last October 20, 2012. The cousins that I remember were Fidel, Lita, Peggy and Bernard. The other relatives were the Ben Parasos from Kaimuki and the Villars from Waipahu. We were particularly close to our two aunts, Nora and another Mary who were single at that time and had many suitors. On some occasions they would go to see Filipino movies and they would bring Norma and me along so we could translate for them.

But most of the time we would go with my Ninong and Ninang to the base theatre. It only cost eight cents to see a movie on base. My Godfather had a car with a rumble seat and that is where Brig and I would sit. These were fun times for us.

At this time I was getting interested in girls and one of my classmates in the sixth grade was Joanne Blakely. Sometimes I would see her at the movie and she would invite me to sit next to her. I would end up holding hands with her and we did a lot of studying together. If ever there was a term for this I would say it was "first love or puppy love".

34

A year later, my mom would give birth to her fourth child, a son and he was named Alohalindo. He was born on July 2, 1948 at Tripler Army Hospital. I remember the fireworks going off in the sky over Pearl Harbor on our way home after picking them up from the hospital. Al, as he is called today, is the only Hawaii-born child of our parents.

Our other adventures in Hawaii included going to the different beaches. Once we were at Keehi Lagoon, a military beach by Honolulu International airport, when my sister Norma, while playing in the water was swept by an unexpected wave to the deep part of the beach. She started screaming and was beginning to sink when Pacifico, Jr. No. 1 dove in and saved her from drowning. I was too far to even make a move and we were so thankful that Pac was actually very close to her to be able to do something about it. On many occasions, we would go with our cousins and relatives around the island stopping at some scenic areas like the Mormon Temple and stopping at any beach for lunch. One of my cousins, Fidel Antonio, Jr. would sometimes spend the weekend with us. He was much older than me and I remember that it was he who taught me how to tell time. I saw him in Hawaii for the last time in 1949 when we left. I didn't see him again until I saw him in San Diego in 1990 when he was living in the San Diego suburbs in a small town called Santee with his family.

I also spent some weekends with the Villars in Waipahu. Leela or grandma is also our grandmother's cousin. My cousins David and Dolly were the ones that would entertain me. My auntie Rose and auntie Nora would also take me shopping and buy clothes for me. It was Leela or grandma who would always cook pinakbet, a Philippine dish of different kinds of vegetables mostly from their garden and always served with fried Spam. You know, I always knew that Hawaii consumes the most Spam in the United States. Our Leela never failed to serve it to us whenever we came to visit them.

Friends from School

In the sixth grade my teacher was Ms. Tom. Some of my classmates who come to mind are Peter Crumpacker, whose father became an admiral in the Navy Supply Corps; Charles Stringfellow, David Shoup, David Ross, whose father would be a shipmate of mine aboard the USS Tecumseh (SSBN-628); David Story, Skippy Moore, Donald Wong, Edward Cleveland, Shirley Johnson, Carol Bow, Constance Smith, and Marjorie Sanderson.

Others who I can recall only by their first name are Rosemarie, Mildred and Natalie. Playmates and neighborhood kids I remember were Ronnie Johnson, Angela Hope, Joanne and Bobbie Blakely, Gene, Linda, Betty and Butch Conger, the son of our Cub Scouts den father. I was also a member of the Junior Police Officer or J P O. Our uniforms were a long sleeved white shirt, long black tie and khaki pants. We directed traffic in front of our school before and after class. We knew a lot of families that we always attended parties with. They were also Navy families. They were: The Lunas, the Cabreras, who had a daughter named Lucy, the Joses with their children Joe and Jolinda, the Ramirezes and their daughter, Millie, The Ramoses family; their son Danny was principal of Marian Catholic High School in Imperial Beach, California and we had a chance to reminisce in 1988. Others were the De Vegas, the Batoons, the Tortonas whose daughter Marrieta was also a crush of mine, the Castanedas whose children were Don, Norma and

Cesar, the Saldanias who became God parents to Lindo and their children were Toto and Connie.

While living in Hawaii, our family car was a Jeep with canvas roof that could be put down. Norma and I would be in the back and Mario was always seated on our mom's lap. There was an incident when we went to see a Filipino movie at Palama Theatre downtown. When we were ready to leave the parking lot, a big dog like a collie jumped in the back with us. We actually had no choice but to give that dog a ride as he would not get off. I do not remember what happened. All I remember was he jumped off our jeep as soon as we reached our house at Moanalua Navy Housing.

Chapter 5

Return to the Philippines

Dad retired from the U.S. Navy after 20 years and decided to return to the Philippines to enroll in school using his GI bill of rights. He already earned his retainer pay. This is equivalent to 75 per cent of his base pay. He would also get paid for going to school. Upon our return to Novaliches, dad decides to enroll at the Manila Law College to take up law. He rented an apartment in Manila and would only come home on weekends. His roommate in the apartment was Artemio Ramil, our cousin, the son of my dad's oldest brother, Lope. Artemio would later on join the U. S. Navy also with the assistance of my father. Art was married to Aurora Halili, a law graduate. They met in college and now live in Huntington Beach. They have five children, Tita, Brynette, Gloria, Arlene and Leonardo or Jojo.

Last October 25 Aurora, Arlene and my wife and I joined our cousins Manuel and Mila Ramil from Philadelphia. We were part of a group that went on a pilgrimage to the Holy Land. We were in Jordan and Jerusalem for twelve days. The four of us spent three days in New York sightseeing in Manhattan and we saw a play on Broadway before flying to Istanbul, Turkey then to Amman, Jordan and taking a bus to Nazareth. I want to add that the day after we left Jerusalem, the Hamas started to fire their missiles there and on the day we left New York for the Holy Land, typhoon Sandy hit Manhattan.

While in law school, my dad was very active in student government. He was president of his class for many terms. He was also very active in the local community. He co-founded the Novaliches Capitol Site Club, whose membership included prominent residents of Novaliches such as Dr. Felipe Roque, Councilor Enrique Ramirez, Dr. Dick Austria, Mr. Mamerto Miranda, Mr. Primo Rivera and many more. He was also involved in the school's Parent Teachers Association. I was a freshman in high school and I enrolled at the Franklin Delano Roosevelt Memorial College or FDRMC. My classmates were Ernesto Santos, Eugenia Ramirez, Teresita Drueco, Lourdes Mojica, Oscar Lucero, Federico Geronimo and Segundo Manese, who after our graduation was able to join the U.S. Coast Guard and I ran into him in San Francisco in late 1980's. Our school was in a building owned by a General Francisco, one of the first generals who graduated from the Philippine Military Academy. He was one of my early idols in Novaliches. I remember he had a booming voice perfect for giving commands. His wife was known as Generala and was involved in many community projects and I secretly admired the whole family.

There were two more additions to our family. A daughter was named after our grandmother. Gregoria was born November 10, 1949. Her name was later changed to Gloria for short. Yes she is now known as Gloria Ramil Omania, Chief of staff to State Senator Tom Torlakson. On September 26, 1951 Cesar was born. Both of them were born at home attended by a local midwife, Lola Putenciana. She was our mom's Godmother. We met her daughter, Virginia, in 2011 when we visited Novaliches with our mom.

Chapter 6

My Teenage Years

I learned to drive a jeep at an early age because my uncle and auntie were engaged in the buy and sell business. You can say they had a route that started from Blumentritt to La Mesa Dam. Yes this is the same dam that my dad helped build. Every day the two of them would drive to Blumentritt to buy groceries which included meat and vegetables and different ingredients. The jeep would be packed at the start and as they proceeded towards Novaliches their customers along the way would just gather around them at their designated stops. By the time they reached our place, they would be about 90% sold out. This is when Eddie and I would take over the driving as my uncle would rest and finish the required paperwork. My aunt would remain doing what she was so good at doing and that is to peddle the rest of her goods to her waiting customers or "suki". Eddie and I would take turns doing the driving and we did this every day until we became very good at it and we knew every policeman in our town. We were able to get away as minors driving without a license and no insurance. At eleven years old I considered myself an expert driver.

My close friends were Ernesto Martin, Celedonio Collado who was one of our groomsman, my cousin, Eddie, Rico Ramirez, the same guy who visited us in Hawaii on their way to the Philippines from Rhode Island, Demetrio Belmes, Boy Ramirez, Mandong Cruz, Cesar Roque and many more. Our gang built a swimming hole in the Tulyahan River by clearing a lot of debris. My uncle gave us an old steel cable and we tied one end on the trunk of a big Tsampoy tree and on the other end we fashioned a wooden handle made from a guava branch. We would swing on the cable and as we were on the deep part, we would do all kinds of acrobatic moves before we would let go of the cable. This was so much fun for us. We called this place "Pasong Choy" for no reason and we did a lot of Tarzan maneuvers using this cable that gave us about a 15 feet drop to about 10 feet deep water. During the rainy season the Tulyahan River would be so swollen that water would almost reach the bridge by our place. This was the perfect time for us to construct a raft made from banana trunks which was plentiful as the wind would knock down many banana trees. We would then gather some trunks and connect them together with kakawate (a plant that grows everywhere in the area) sticks and then tie them with a rope. This would be strong enough to hold the banana trunks together and act as a raft enough for about four people to ride the current of the swollen river. We would start from the bridge which was at Tabing Ilog, (riverstde) in Novaliches and end up at Pasong Choy, close to the town of Kaybiga, about 10 miles downstream. This is also the same river where I learned how to swim because I fell in and I learned because of fear. I also taught my brother, Mario, how to swim using the same method. These were exciting times for us and even today Fred or Rico and I would reminisce about our adventures in the river.

During this time my dad graduated from law school but he was not able to take the Philippine bar exam as he retained his U.S. citizenship. He just devoted his time in several business ventures like poultry farming, tilapia raising, a poultry supply store and juke boxes. I was the one who attended maintenance training for our juke boxes and so that was my duties. I was going to school in the evening and in the day time I would take care of our juke boxes which included minor repairs, replacing the records and dealing with the business owners and actually counting the money for dividing and giving the profit to my mom. We placed three juke boxes into the three cafes in our town and they were all trying to compete with each other for customers. We did very well because this was very new to our town and many young suitors would play the appropriate record hoping that their loved one would hear the music. I was then courting Rosemarie Susano, the daughter of the owner of Novaliches Market. Once we went to a movie in Manila and on our way home when we boarded the bus, her mother was also on board the same bus. She became very angry and was raising her voice so I decided to get off and I waited for the next one. I was worried because I overheard her say she was going to tell my father. She was a teacher in the elementary school where my father was the PTA president. It even crossed my mind that I may be forced to marry Rosemarie. I did not hear anything from my father and I continued seeing her.

Before long we were able to buy the two lots adjacent to ours. One lot is where we started our poultry farm. In the other lot he built a small commercial building and one of our cousins started a barber shop. Today that lot has a bank building but it does not belong to us anymore. Then my dad leased one rice paddy from a Mr. Pedro Valenzuela, a friend of his, which he converted into a fishpond. The government had a program and was just starting to introduce the tilapia fish to the country. They provided free seedlings to anyone that had a pond and we were the first one to have a tilapia pond in Novaliches. Dad even had a small concrete pond in the side of our house where we also had tilapia for our home consumption. It was so cool to cast your pole and the fishes would bite it instantly. Most of the time we would have burning ambers for instant fish barbeque.

Chapter 7

Meeting my Future Bride

One summer, I was invited by my cousin, Benjamin Ramil, to join him for the weekend in Baguio, the summer capital of the Philippines. At that time Manong Ben was a sanitary inspector for the city of Caloocan. Before that, when he was still in school, he lived with us and was our official driver as we owned a car that my dad bought from his cousin in Hawaii. It was a black 1948 Buick. I would sit in that car and listen to the radio but I was not allowed to drive it by any means. On our way to Baguio and upon arriving at Tarlac, we decided to stop by Carinio to visit our grandfather who has been a widower since we lost our grandmother, Maria Apuan Ramil, during the war. We were surprised to find out that there was a party going on.

One of our cousins, Paterno Yanos, was having a baptismal party for his child. That was really a good break for us as we were both hungry after being in the bus for over two hours and it was already lunch time. Paterno's sister, Ruthelda Yanos lived with us in Novaliches. She was our mom's help in taking care of my younger brothers and sisters. We call her Manang Ruthie, the daughter of our aunt, Valentina. Ruthie is now Mrs. Baculanta and lives with her family in San Marcos, California. While eating I was seated across from one of the child's sponsors. She was particularly beautiful in a red dress. I found out later that she was one of the candidates for Miss Paniqui who would reign during the town fiesta.

Her name was Miss Teresita Obcena Roxas. I told her that my name was Quintin Ramil, Jr. and that Patring is my first cousin and that I am a law student and we are on our way to Baguio with my cousin, Ben. I said that I would like to know her better and asked her if I could write to her. Better yet I asked her if she could join us next week end to go to the town of Pance to attend a memorial celebration for my uncle, Pedro Ramil, who passed away the year before. She said that she would ask her parents. I made sure that my cousins who knew her parents would put in a few encouraging words for me so that they would allow their daughter to come with us

We boarded a bus for Pance but the bus only went as far as Ramos. From here we would have to catch another bus or wait for a horse drawn kalesa or karetela. There were no karetelas in sight so we had to walk the rest of the way. There must have been more than ten of us in the group and the walk was too long and the sun was beating down on us. What made it bearable for me was once in a while I would get to talk to Tere. I even bragged that the next time I come to Pance I would be driving and not walking. This became true because in 1966 I was able to get stationed in San Miguel, Zambales at the U.S. Naval Communications Station Philippines and we brought with us our car, a white and blue 1965 two door hard top Chevrolet, a Malibu SS model which we bought in New London, Connecticut.

The memorial service was very moving and there was a great deal of food. After dinner, the youths had group singing and ended up playing different parlor games. Each one was encouraged to introduce their favorite game. I volunteered and I introduced the "guess the number game," where I would turn my back and I asked the group to think of a group number between one and ten. Once they decided on a particular number I would then randomly cup their faces pretending I was reading the number in their eyes. I would go to many participants and when I cupped my cousin, Ben, he would give me the signal by grinding his teeth giving me the group number. I would pretend to go around again and when I cupped Tere's face I had the urge to continue holding it and I wanted so bad to pull her face towards my lips. This I did not do but announced what the number was. They were all surprised and continued the laughter as it must been funny the way I was trying to cup many faces but pretending I was not getting any readings.

Chapter 8

Leaving for the U.S.

We were going to have a despedida party at home and so my mom began the planning. This was the time when our life was settled down and my dad's different businesses were booming. We had a Lanzones tree (similar to a luquat) in our backyard that had one bunch of fruit. My mom planted this tree when she was pregnant with me. It was the first thing she added to the property after acquiring it. It took 18 years before this lanzones tree began to have flowers as it is uncommon for this particular tree to even survive in a place like Novaliches. Most lanzones thrives in the provinces of Laguna, Batangas and sometimes Cavite. That is why my mother said we would not pick the fruits of our tree. We will just look and admire it until it falls off or until it was time for the party. My mom's cousin Kakang Martin Bautista was walking around our backyard when he spotted the lanzones bunch. He did not hesitate picking it as it was already very ripe. He started eating it and proudly announced to everyone around of his feat. When I realized what had happened I just limped and could not utter a word. I looked at my mother and my siblings who were also mesmerized to what we witnessed. I was so mad but only blamed myself for not putting up a sign or anything to discouraged anyone who would get close to our lanzones tree.

Kakang Martin Bautista is the father of my cousin Rosie Pineda. Her husband, Manuel Pineda was in the business of raising roosters used in cock fighting. He was

Breeder of the Year several times in the Philippines as well as our other cousin, Fernando Reyes, who has a farm in Lipa City, Batangas. He was also Breeder of the Year once or twice.

Our house and two residential lots including all our businesses were sold to my uncle Tayong. We were paid twenty thousand pesos equivalent to ten thousand dollars as the exchange at that time was two to one. The contract to purchase stipulated that we had the option of buying back our property. The main reason our dad decided to migrate to America was to give us, his children the opportunity for a better life. I always had the perception that in America, money grows on trees. The other reason is that I was already eighteen. I could no longer be his dependent and I had to earn U.S. citizenship on my own.

My dad was also tired of the way the Philippine government was being run. Graft and corruption were everywhere and you had to know someone before you could get served in any office you go to unless you pay someone. Hey wait, that is still true today! There is no change. It is so difficult to hear someone say, "May I help you?" We were booked on another MSTS (Military Ship Transportation Service) ship. This time it was the USNS General Patrick. There was one drawback because we were travelling on space availability only. The spaces for my mother and my siblings were only good up to Hawaii. My dad and I transferred below decks and rode with the troops for the trip to Port Hueneme, which is the Sea Bees base. They were returning to their home base after constructing the runways of Naval Air Station Cubi Point. During this leg I met an American named Joe Black, who lives in Mira Mesa. We currently both attend the same church and he is married to a Filipina, named Connie.

My mom, Norma, Mario, Alohalindo, Gloria and Cesar, due to unavailability of cabin space, had to disembark in Hawaii. They were met at the pier by our uncle, Mr. Ben Paraso, our dad's cousin. They stayed with him at their house in Kaimuki until they were able to book their flight to San Francisco. When they arrived in San Francisco, they were met by my ninong and ninang, (Godparents) Mr. And Mrs. Brigido Tamayo and they stayed at their home in Vallejo, California. Meanwhile my dad and I were berthed with the troops below decks. With us was a group of Philippine Boy Scouts that were to attend a Scout Jamboree somewhere in the mid-west. They were given free ride by the United States government. I regret the fact that I did not seriously try to make friends with any of them even though we were berthed next to each other. I later learned that some of these scouts would go to another jamboree in Greece. On the way home, their plane crashed. Later they were honored by the Quezon City council by naming streets after them.

Upon arrival in Southern California, my dad and I boarded a Greyhound bus for Vallejo, California. We were met by my very kind ninong Brigido Tamayo. To tell you how kind they were, our family, consisting of my dad, mom and six children, lived with them for four months, in a three bedroom one bath house. I was the only one that slept in another bedroom with my God brother, Brig. The rest of my family stayed in one bedroom. Timing was everything. We became experts in knowing when to use the bathroom for our daily existence, and of course, we tried to be as unobtrusive as we could possibly be. Brig worked at a local farm, and I was able to work alongside him. He introduced me to the foreman as another worker and he asked if I knew how to pick fruit. I replied "yes sir". Lucky for us it was still summer and there were many fruits to be picked in the nearby farms. There were many jobs if you were not picky.

Joining Brig and me, was a family friend, Julius Fernandez. We had to carry a wooden ladder, reinforced with metal brackets, along each orchard row. It was very heavy. I was questioned by the field boss if I could carry it, as he was worried I might not be able to keep up with the rest of the pickers. We were assigned a row of trees and given a metal ring shaped like a figure eight. The small ring would go to the middle finger and we place the big ring in the bottom of the fruit. If it did not fall through the ring, then it was big enough to be picked. This is how table pears are determined whether or not they may be harvested. As we approach the pear tree, we placed the ladder as close as possible to the center of the tree. Then we would climb it and begin picking fruit and using the ring to measure. If it was the right size it was placed in a bag draped over our shoulder. I would not bother moving my ladder as when I got on top I could carefully move about picking most of the fruits using my talent in tree climbing. I got so good at this that I would even beat the group and finished first most of the time. I had to prove to the boss that I could handle it. After the first day, the boss checked my work. He wasn't a man of many words, but he gave me thumbs up and I could tell he was happy with my work. I was accepted as a regular picker. In the evening is when I would feel the pain and aches in my body. I was not really used to this kind of work. This also holds true for my father. We already had it made in the Philippines. My dad's different businesses were doing very well. So what made him decide to find a better place for us in America?

In some ranches that grow prunes, they allowed the whole family to pick. The prune trees were loaded with fruits. It takes a shaker and a beater to get the fruits to fall to

52

the ground where it is gathered by the gatherers. My dad and I would be the shakers and we also would beat the tree with a big stick until all the fruits fell to the ground. This is where my siblings would take over. They would gather the plums and placed them in boxes with our number on it where it would be placed in the tractor. It was almost like a game for the children. We had fun and got paid doing it. What a deal!

Chapter 9

From Stockton to the U.S. Navy

Early Life in Stockton

In September 1956 I enrolled at Vallejo Junior College for an Associate Degree as my law school transcript had to be evaluated before I could enroll in a law school. This was not practical so I simply continued taking courses and at the same time I enlisted in the U.S. Navy Reserves. I joined a submarine unit at Mare Island Naval Base and was sent to Submarine School at Hunters Point Naval Shipyard in San Francisco where I attended SP (Submarine Prospect) and SG (Submarine Graduate) school.

On weekends I would be invited by the base librarian, Mrs. Soledad Fernandez, to spend the weekend with her family in Berkeley. Auntie Solie, as we knew her, is the sister of my dad's cumpadre, Pacifico Jose. She is also a very close friend of my Ninang Petronilla Tamayo. This was a blessing for me as I did not have enough money to go home to Stockton so I would just spend my time in the barracks. Joining the Fernandez family was a special treat for me. Auntie Solie would cook for us and I became very close to her children Jules, Lito and Sol. Sometimes her family would be invited to some Filipino parties and I would be with them. She also gave us a lot of hand-me-down clothes which I wore. This was very nice because since our arrival in California, when I started working in the farms picking fruits, all my salaries were given directly to my mom except for $20 which I used to buy a new jacket. Auntie Solie was a special lady who treated me as her own son.

One of the reservists in my class was John Jenkins from San Diego. He was to become my shipmate on the USS Tunny SSG-282. Today we are still friends and attend our ship's reunion every other year. Oin May 29, 1957 our youngest brother was born at the Mare Island Naval Hospital. He was named Michael, I believe, at a suggestion from one of the nurses who helped my mom deliver.

My dad continued to work on the farms while waiting for a job. He followed the picking season which took him from Suisun to Stockton and other outlying areas. My dad was not used to this kind of work. He did not give us any hint that he did not like what he was doing, but was always on the lookout for a better paying job. He finally found work at the Veterans Hospital in Livermore, in the kitchen staff. I would drive him to work on Sunday evenings and pick him up on Friday nights. He only spent the week-end with us. We only had one car and the family needed it most which is the reason I ended up driving him to and from Livermore. That car was a standard 1953 Pontiac sedan, which my father bought for $700. The proceeds of the sale of our property in the Philippines were slowly being depleted as it was used for the down payment of our house. I needed to get a job of my own to be able to help the family. As it stood, I could only work on weekends picking grapes, onions or asparagus in the Stockton area. I made several friends working in the farms. They were: Rudy Omania, the brother of my future brother-in-law, Louie Omania, Ken and Ben Gonzales, Ted Candelaria, Conrado Bernardo, Briccio De Castro and Tito Tana, whose uncle, Leo was sometimes our foreman.

Dad soon decided to buy a house in Stockton as this is the center of the farmlands where he worked. I remember the realtor showing us different homes in the area. The realtor must have been a rookie because he was showing us homes in the northern part of town where no Filipinos, Asians, Mexicans or Blacks owned a home.

In Stockton everything north of Charter Way was considered the white area and everything south was the non-white area. I am sure that when my dad made the offer to purchase the house, discrimination was the last thing on his mind. When our realtor tried to back out of the deal my dad maintained our rights in buying the house. That was our first experience with discrimination. After all, this was 1957 and the Civil Rights act has not yet been passed by Congress. Driving around Stockton I soon realized that there is such a thing as discrimination. But soon the neighbors began to know us; especially the kids and they welcomed us into the neighborhood. My brothers and sisters were enrolled in the area public schools and Norma and I were enrolled at Stockton College. I know that Mario and Lindo had their own paper route and made a lot of friends. They used their bikes delivering newspapers. Our commisary store is the one at the Rough and Ready Island. We would only go there when our dad was home and sometimes we needed other items but we had to wait.

Being Active Duty in the US Navy

I reported to Naval Station, Treasure Island to be processed and to wait for transportation to Hawaii. On weekends I would come home sometimes wearing my uniform. You see, deep inside me, I always had the desire to be in the U.S. Navy. As a matter of fact, my prayers every night always included the words, "And please God make me grow taller so that I can qualify to join the Navy." Now my prayers were answered.

Our plane landed at Hickam Air Force Base and we were met by a Navy bus that took us to the different ships tied up along the piers. I was taken to the Submarine base where the USS Tunny SSG-282 was tied up on Pier One. The Topside watch met me and welcomed me to the ship. After logging me in, he instructed me to report to the submarine barracks about a block away where I was assigned a bunk and a locker. I would have two bunks, one in the barracks and one aboard the sub. On our duty days, we had to stay on board and of course when we were off we stayed in the barracks. This was one leisure that we had over the sailors on the surface ships across the harbor from us. I was given liberty that afternoon and I did not waste any time. I called my uncle, Ben Paraso, and had dinner with the family that evening. It did not take long for me to renew my acquaintances with my cousins, Almo, Carlo and Cynthia. It had been 1949 when we saw each other last.

The following day, I met the Chief-of-the-Boat (COB). He is considered the most senior enlisted man on board a submarine. This position is unique only to the submarine service. He works directly under the direction of the Executive Officer, the second in-charge of command. His assigned duties are the upkeep of the ship externally, the assignments of personnel to the different watches, ashore or at sea, maintenance of supplies and common spaces like the showers, bathrooms, berthing compartments, everything topside including the superstructure. I was assigned to the Deck Force, which means I would work for the Leading Seaman and we all worked for the Chief of the Boat. You guessed it. I was given a scrapper, the tool we used to scrape rust off metal to prepare it for painting. This was a continuous cycle whenever the sub is in port. We had to look good externally and internally.

The ship is always being prepared for painting by means of scrapping rusts and barnacles wherever it may be. It is then primed and sprayed with haze gray paint. I also learned how to make heaving lines, monkey's fists and how to tie a bowline. I became an expert in the use of spray painting equipment and learned how to order supplies. I also got a Navy driver's license as part of my duties was to be the driver when in port.

We operated out at sea on a daily basis and I learned how to steer the ship, man the bow planes, which controls the depth and the stern planes which control the angle of the ship as it runs underwater. When on the surface, I learned how to be a lookout. We report contacts by bearings in degrees: directly ahead is 000 and to the right is 090, to the left is 270 and directly aft is 180, and so on.

After a year in the Deck Force, I became the leading seaman which means I got to supervise 8 to 10 personnel. Once I gave an order to one of my men but he ignored me and even started calling me names. I got so mad that I chased him with a scrapper. When the COB saw this he put his arms around me and told me to stop. It was then that he called me "Tiger", a name that would stick with me for the rest of my time on the Tunny. The mission of our submarine was to carry two Regulus missiles housed in a hangar behind the sail. Tunny was the first firing missile submarine. We normally operated with two other subs, the USS Cusk and the USS Carbonero which acted as our guidance support. After we fired the missile, we guided it for about 200 miles towards the forward sub. It takes over guidance of the missile toward the sub nearest the target where it would take over and guide the missile toward the target. When it is above the target, it dumps it and the missile hits the objective. This was how the early missile subs operated. One drawback was the submarine has to be on the surface before it can launch its missiles and it took more than one submarine to hit a target 600 miles away. Today, our nuclear powered missile firing submarines carries more than 16 missiles each and they remain submerged while launching. Each missile is already pre-set. It knows where it is and it knows where it is going. You just have to let it go. No guidance required.

I made a trip to the disbursing office and made an allotment to my mother. I knew that my family could use all the help that we can get. My base pay was only $86 a month but the allotment to my mother was for $100 a month. It is a blessing that I was stationed aboard a submarine which made me entitled to Hazardous Duty Pay and Sea Pay. I continued this allotment until our first son was born.

Hawaii was a great place to be stationed especially for a Filipino like me. There are so many restaurants that cater to us. One of the pleasures we look forward to is to go to town and eat at a Filipino restaurant where the food is almost like what mom used to cook. My friends and I would do this almost every payday. I remember that in one of the restaurants we patronized, the owner had a very pretty niece that sometimes helped in serving the food. Her name was Thelma, and she had so many sailor suitors that whatever intentions I had, I completely erased them from my mind.

Then we began meeting Filipino families and one such family was the Paguios. Their house was like a receiving station for us. We would always be welcome to

60

stay, sometimes overnight. But the best part was that we were welcome to prepare home cooked meals. In those days it was so easy for us to ask our cooks in the sub for food to take off the ship. It was not unusual for us to just get a hunk of prime rib or several pounds of steaks. My friends at this time were Max and Zeny Paguio, Romy Esteban, Armando Carlos, Romy Valerio, Romeo Andaleon, Anita and Bea. I was writing to Teresita Roxas all along but somehow, I really do not know what happened, she sent me a picture of her wearing a nun's outfit. My thinking was, she joined and became a nun or a sister. I then became very close to Zeny and also met many other girls on the other side of the island. One of them was Julie Sacramento. Her sister, Nora, was dating a friend of mine, Ernie Rimando. They eventually got married and still live in Hawaii today.

62

Chapter 10

Tahiti and My God-Brother Brig

Tunny Goes to Tahiti

My submarine's schedule was to go on Regulus patrol by sailing north all the way to the Aleutian Islands. Sometimes we would stop by Kodiak Island or at Adak Island to fuel. Adak is famous for its National Forest. There were four trees on the whole island. Someone said that there is a woman behind every tree in the island. I did not see anyone. After four patrols we received orders to go south to the French Polynesian Islands of Tahiti. We would be the first U.S. ship to ever visit Tahiti. To reach Tahiti, we must first cross the Equator. This is where sailors who have crossed before are called "Shellbacks". And those who have not are called "Pollywogs". The initiation is very colorful. The Royal Family consisted of Neptunus Rex or king; there is a Queen, a Royal Baby, usually the one with the biggest belly as the Pollywogs are made to kiss his belly, and Davey Jones, the Royal Scribe. Neptunus Rex and the Royal Scribe are the two signatories to the certificate and shellback cards that are presented to the new shellbacks after the initiation. We crossed the equator twice that day, submerged on one and the other on the surface where the initiation took place topside. The shellbacks on board had it all planned. They have been saving our garbage since the day we left Pearl Harbor. It was placed in a canvass chute and hidden in the storage locker below decks. They also had chopped up rubber hoses about three feet long that they would use to beat us as we crawled through the chute. After surviving the crawling through the garbage while being beaten with a hose, we would then follow individual orders.

The first order of business for me was I had to report to the Royal Barber where I was given a royal trim or no hair. As a matter of fact, we pollywogs received the same kind of haircut. Next we were given a concoction to drink. It was so bitter and spicy hot that I almost threw up. We were also given the order to kiss the royal tummy every time we hear the word "Pollywog". Chief Wineberg played the part of Neptunus Rex. Chief Davis was the Royal Baby. J. D. Crowley was Davy Jones and Mr. Shaeffer was the Royal Queen and they were all dressed for the occasion. I will never forget Chief Wineberg and Crowley as they signed my card which I still carry in my wallet today. As a matter of fact, I have two cards. The second one was from the USS Tecumseh SSBN 628. There were only 12 of us shellbacks and we had to initiate more than 100 pollywogs. This time I played the part of Davy Jones and I signed more than 100 cards. Could it be that there is someone out there with a card in their wallet with my signature?

In 1970 I enrolled at San Diego City College. On the first day of class our professor was taking muster as he checked our seat location. After my name was called, he approached me and threw a card on my desk. He said that he has been carrying his card since he got out of the Navy and that he will never forget my name as he was onboard the Tecumseh with me and we initiated him. I of course, signed his card.

We arrived in Tahiti and tied up right in front of the market place in Papaete, the capital. A huge crowd met us, as it was the first time for them to see a U.S. submarine. After securing the lines, I ended up having the first topside watch, which means I had to be in my dressed whites and looking squared away, with a belt, holster and a 45 caliber pistol in my waist. I was responsible for the security of the ship and also the direct representative of the Commanding Officer. People were staring at me and some were trying to talk to me in French, which is one of the languages spoken there. I noticed a very attractive girl drive up on a Lambretta scooter. She smiled at me and waved. I waved back and also smiled. She was beautiful. She approached me and asked if she could see the submarine. I told her that if she can wait for another two hours I would personally escort her and give her a tour. She said she would come back. At this time, the duty electricians were busy setting up a movie for showing later in the evening. The screen was on our sail and the projector on the pier. Two thirds of our crew were already on the beach at various bars. They told me that in the beginning, the ladies did not want to get near them. We found out later on that our original shellbacks were spreading the word around to the ladies in the bars that if they see U.S. sailors with real short haircut that they should stay away from them as they have VD.

The MGM crew was shooting the film, "Mutiny on the Bounty" in Papeete the same time the Tunny was there and many of our crew members were cast as extras in the movie. Even Marlon Brando came on board for dinner as an invited guest of our captain. Before long I was relieved of my watch but I had to stay on board as I was in the duty section. Soon Miriam Prokop arrived in her scooter and saw me right away. She just came to me and I motioned her to follow me. I introduced myself as Ram, my other name on board, and we proceeded to climb down the ladder in the

Forward Torpedo Room. Here I showed her the torpedoes and the tubes we used to fire them from. Then we went to the Forward Battery compartment. This is where the officers berthing and dining room is located.

At the control room is where everything is controlled and I showed her the different watch stations. The bow and stern planes, different valves and the steering helm is directly above the control room which is the Conning Tower. She was just smiling all along. When we arrived at the After Battery compartment where the dining room and galley is located, I had her sit in one of the booths. I then went down to our chill box, got some ice cream and cookies and we just sat there eating and talking. I found out that her father is from Czechoslovakia and her mother is Tahitian. She has a brother in Paris studying and two sisters at home one older than her and one younger than her. She agreed to meet me the next day and we would go on her scooter and she promised to show me the island. Meanwhile she would stay and watch the movie with me. She was also an extra in the movie, Mutiny in the Bounty, as a dancer. She was a very good friend of Tarita, the leading lady whom Marlon Brando married.

We went around the island in her Lambretta scooter. I sat behind her as she maneuvered the scooter and made our way all over the island. At times I found myself hanging on for dear life. I had to be in uniform as we were not allowed to have civilian clothes aboard our sub. I had to hold my hat and my neckerchief as it was blowing all over. Miriam was good at her driving and of course knew her way around. I was getting the thrill of my life by just hanging on to her waist. I hardly noticed the beauty and serenity of Tahiti. We stopped at a water hole. Actually it was the mouth of the river complete with a small waterfall with very lush greenery. It was not difficult to get lost in this kind of surroundings. She was wearing red pants and a white tank top but inside she had on her bathing suit. She asked me if I wanted to swim and fool me I declined, as I did not have any swimming trunks.

We ended up at her place and I was introduced to her family, but first we went back to my ship and I invited my two shipmates with me as Miriam had two sisters. We had a wonderful dinner prepared by her mother. In the evening, Mr. Prokop and his daughters played musical instruments and the girls danced several Tahitian dances. I presented Miriam's dad with a brand new Navy Issue raincoat. I do not remember how we got back to our ship but that night was a very memorable evening for me. I promised Miriam that I would write to her as soon as we return to Hawaii. We exchanged several letters. In 1964 she became Miss Tahiti and was featured in Playboy magazine. Later on I read in a magazine that she married an executive with the Pepsi cola company.

Brig Meets Nancy

In May of 1961 I received orders to attend RM "A" school in San Diego, California. Our family was now living in Livermore after selling our house in Stockton. The last time I was home was two years earlier when I took leave in Stockton. I had just re-enlisted and with the reenlistment money I was able to buy a used car for Norma so she did not have to drive dad to work. On leave again before reporting to my school, I visited my Ninong and Ninang in Vallejo and discovered that Brig was also there. He had plans on driving down to San Diego as his parents just bought him a brand new black 1961 Impala convertible. Our plan was he will pick me up from Livermore and together we would drive down to San Diego. On the way we would stop and visit friends. My Ninang had a long talk with me while I was visiting. She said she heard that I have a Filipina girlfriend and that I should find someone for Brig. I promised her I would try.

The night before I was to leave, my father confided to me that he had a daughter, born during the war that is possibly living in San Diego. Needless to say, I was shocked to hear about this for the very first time. No wonder I heard my mom arguing with my dad recently in the middle of the night when all the children were asleep.

This is one thing I remember very well. Our parents never quarreled in front of us. My father sat me down and explained in details his experience during the war. He honestly believed that his family perished during the bombing of Manila. He just assumed that my mom and I were casualties when the Japanese started bombing Manila as his crippled submarine slowly escaped to Australia. Later on he was assigned to the Navy Commissary store in Panama. There he met Inah, a young lovely Panamanian. Because of the war situation, most Panamanians were dependent on the Americans for economical support. He lived with Inah and she bore him a child, a daughter whom they named Gwen. After the war, he learned through the Red Cross that we were alive. He immediately requested duty to the Philippines and was lucky enough to be assigned to the Philippine Sea Frontier Command in Pasay City, Philippines. Before he left Panama, He remembered Gwen walking with him and was running after him holding an ice cream cone. He entrusted the care of his partner and daughter to one of his close friends and member of his crew, Petty Officer second class Manuel Archuleta. Mr. Archuleta in turn married Inah and adopted

Gwen, their only child. When he retired from the U.S. Navy, they settled in San Diego.

Brig picked me up in Livermore and the two of us proceeded to drive down south to San Diego. We stopped in La Mirada, just south of LA, as I wanted to see an old flame of mine, whom I met in Hawaii. They stopped there on their way to California as their father became ill. The father was admitted to Tripler Army Hospital and they stayed with their relatives, the Abadilla family. It was nice to see Myrna again. She is so full of laughter, very funny and loves telling jokes. Their mother, Aling Toyang, remembered me as well and invited us to stay for dinner and we were welcomed to stay and rest before we return to our driving. Aling Toyang prepared a very delicious meal which we greatly appreciated.

After dinner, I noticed a picture of their other daughter and I showed it to Brig. We found out that Myrna's older sister, Nancy, was in the Waves but will be getting out soon. She was presently assigned in New York. Brig became very interested as we also found out that it won't be long before she is discharged from the Navy and she will be arriving in San Francisco and most likely would be met by their cousins living in Alameda. We ended up staying overnight. I already asked Myrna to keep me informed of her sister's plans as we both wanted for the two of them to meet. Brig got her phone number and that night they were able to talk to each other. That same year Brig and Nancy got married. Before the wedding, Nancy's friend, Tessie Galang, arrived from New York where she was attending a fashion school. The four of us went to San Francisco and had dinner there. I learned that Tessie's family owned a fashion school in Manila called Madonna's Fashion School. At the wedding reception, I caught the bride's garter, which meant I would be the next to get married. I made sure I had the phone number of Madonna's in Manila. Actually Tessie Galang gave me a note for her mother. In June 2012 Brig and Nancy celebrated their 50th wedding anniversary at the Mandalay Bay in Las Vegas. Present were my wife and I, and Roger and Tessie Biglang-awa. They have two daughters and three grandchildren. The older daughter, Nancy Stella lives in Los Angeles with her son, Bryce. Their younger daughter, Stephanie is married to Ron Rivera. They have two children. Their son, Christopher, is with Disneyland and their daughter, Courtney is a sophomore at UCLA and plays for the womens softball team. She is one of their star pitchers. Today Ron is the head football coach of the Carolina Panthers of the NFL and was named coach of the year. Before this he was the defensive coordinator for the San Diego Chargers. I got to see many pre-season games. Thanks to Ron and Stephanie for those freebies.

Chapter 11

Meeting Gwen

The night before leaving Livermore I had a long talk with my dad. He asked me if I could try to look for the Archuleta family and to try to meet Gwen. He suggested that I ask the Jose family. After checking in at the Naval Training Center, San Diego, California, I began calling old family friends in the area. Lucky for me, Jolinda Jose, the older sister of Pacifico, Jr. (Jr. #1 in Hawaii) worked at the Navy Public Works Center not very far from my school.

The family invited me to spend the weekend with them and that Jolinda would pick me up. Jolinda and I were both very glad to see each other as we were neighbors in Hawaii earlier and we both liked going to the movies and we both kept a scrap book about movie stars famous at that time. In other words, we had something in common. On our way to their home, I asked her if she knew a Gwen Archuleta, which she did and as a matter of fact they are both members of the Filipino Youth Club of San Diego, a club which she suggested I also join since I will be in the area for a while. The next meeting would be this Sunday and she also suggested that I join them. My feeling was I hit the jackpot and I was able to tell my dad of the situation. He would eagerly wait for my report without informing my mom. In a way I feel guilty conspiring with my dad but I truly understand where he was coming from. My mother on the other hand was so devastated in knowing that my father had an illegitimate child during their marriage. I tend to believe that my father honestly thought that we were victims of the Japanese bombings of Manila. Is that because males tend to stick together or the macho in me that made me feel this way?

Early Sunday morning I was already apprehensive. Just the thought of meeting my sister for the first time made me feel uneasy. I know that it took a while before I finally got some sleep. I could hardly wait to meet her. But I really did not know how I was going act when I saw her.

Soon we were on our way to the meeting at someone's house. I acted very cool when we entered the house and of course I was being introduced to everyone but my mind and my eyeballs were wondering around looking for Gwen. It was a good thing that we got there first. This would give me the opportunity to see her as she approached us. I sat by the window making sure I had a clear view of the street and the entrance to the house.

Before long a car stopped and sure enough I heard someone say Gwen is here. I was looking at her from the window trying to figure out exactly how she looked and studying her every move. And when I finally saw her in front of me, I felt a feeling I cannot describe. She had a mole by her upper lip very similar to my dad's and her beauty was similar to a Spanish mestiza or perhaps Panamanian. I learned later on that she was a candidate for Miss Philippines of San Diego, sponsored by the Philippine community. I grabbed her hand during our introduction but I really wanted to hug her. It felt like I knew her all along. I was really trying to show her how happy I was to be meeting her and I really sensed that the feeling was mutual. I began calling her in the evenings. We were always talking about something but I held off telling her who I really was. I was known as Ramy from my last name but I did not bother telling her this. She

72

just called me Ramy like everyone else. Soon we were talking almost every evening. It was Friday and she invited me to go her place so I could meet her parents. She was about to leave her office when her boss asked her to work overtime. She had no way of getting in touch with me so she called her mother and told her that someone was coming and to just explain to me that she would be late and I was welcome to wait. That is what happened, I arrived and I was welcomed by Mr. and Mrs. Archuleta. I was offered coffee and we were exchanging pleasantries when Mr. Archuleta asked me about my parents. Before this, my dad would always tell me to get to know the family and then to introduce myself and hopefully someday I could take Gwen to see him. He was even concerned if Gwen needed help financially. When Mr. Archuleta again asked me where my parents live....I showed him my Navy identification card.

He could not help see my picture and full name. I very respectfully said, Sir, Ma'am, you know my father. I am Quintin Ramil, Jr. That is when I saw the anguished look on Mr. Archuleta's face. His face turned white and he began to cry. He placed his hands on my shoulder and said, son I have to ask you a very special favor. My daughter does not know any other father. I am asking you now to promise me, while I am still alive to never ever tell Gwen that I am not her father. Can you promise me this? At that point I was also in tears and I kept nodding my head...yes sir, yes sir, I said repeatedly. Inah was speechless.

I continued my relationship with Gwen. It even came to the point that she thought I had other intentions. One time around Christmas, Mario came down to San Diego with my brother-in-law, Carlos Matro, who dropped Mario off at our apartment I was sharing with Brig and Cesar Ambalada. Carlos went to his new assignment. The gang decided to attend a midnight mass, a tradition that the Filipinos continued doing even in California. When we arrived at the crowded church, my brother, Mario ended up sitting next to Gwen. I did not notice this right away until it was time to say the Lord's Prayer and the congregation were holding hands. Mario was holding hands with our sister that particular mass and I was the only one that knew.

On to Radioman "A" School

I reported to my school and the first thing that happened was I met two Filipino sailors both First Class. They were RM1 Tony Zolina and YN1 Tony Marquez. I later learned that Tony Marquez is a cousin of Nancy Doloiras, the future Mrs. Brig Tamayo. RM1 Zolina was one of my instructors and Tony Marquez was in charge of the administration office. Tony Marquez nominated me to be the Class Petty Officer of my class, which means I had to march my class to and from the galley and I was the Chief's main assistant. This was a ritual at all the schools on base. At 11:30 the whole school goes into formation and each class according to seniority begins to march towards the chow hall. The most senior or graduating class is the model and each Class Petty Officer has a unique way of giving the preparatory and executes command. I got to be very good at this and even if we were the most junior, I made sure my command was loud and clear and the timing perfect. I was also so conscious of my accent. I enjoyed this early recognition and just hoped that I could also prove myself capable academically.

Our class won the "Most Outstanding Class of 1961". I also began playing golf as Tony Zolina was a golfer and he was willing to teach me the game in exchange for baby sitting their children on Friday or Saturday evenings. I enjoyed the game of golf so much and soon was hooked as a golfer. Tony was a good instructor, not only in communications procedures, but also in the game of golf. We enjoyed playing the Navy courses in the area.

In those days there were not many Filipinos playing golf and so whenever Tony and I played, the other golfers would always give us a second look. The only Filipinos that I would see on the golf course were pulling not a cart but a hose. At this time there was a Philippine Navy crew training in San Diego as they will be the one to man the U.S Navy destroyer that the United States was giving to the Philippine Navy. I met some that were assigned to my school. They were Petty Officers Damaso and Corsame.

I graduated in the top three of my class and also made Third Class Petty Officer and my orders were to the USS Queenfish AGSS-393 home ported in San Diego. I reported aboard my new ship which was tied up at Broadway pier downtown and I quickly found out that our ship was scheduled to visit several Asian countries, including the Philippines. I was so happy and could hardly wait for us to get underway.

The day finally arrived and soon we would be in Asian waters. The first port that we visited was Bangkok, Thailand. We just went up the long river and tied up in Bangkok where we did mostly touring and shopping. We went to the floating market and experienced some night life in the city. We were also given a tour of the palace. The second port we went to was Nha Trang, Vietnam. This was before the Vietnam War began. We were considered U.S. advisors and we were scheduled to tie up near their Naval

Academy to train their midshipman about submarine operations. Nha Trang is a beautiful city with many French influences. The pier where we docked was next to a big park very similar to Luneta Park in Manila. We held open house for the public and I met several Filipino Overseas Workers, mostly in the construction field.

We were invited to visit their camp and so my shipmate, Abundio Maliwanag and I got on a tricycle and went to the Filipino camp as guests of a couple from Batangas whom we met earlier. When we arrived at the camp we saw so many Filipinos who were also eager to see us in U.S. Navy sailor uniforms. They prepared many Filipino dishes for us. I met an elderly Filipino from my hometown of Novaliches. As a matter of fact, his wife is my mother's cumadre. They have a stall at our market. I personally know his wife and children, but had never met Mr. Goding Palma before. When we were leaving, Mr. Palma asked me if I could deliver a small bag to his family which I brought back with me to our ship. Our submarine conducted daily operations with the Vietnamese Navy and to make sure we had good communications, two U. S. Sailors, a radioman and a sonar man would ride the Vietnamese ship. I ended up riding the Vietnamese ship several times and I did most of the communications with my ship as communicated by their captain who was the only one who spoke English.

Our next schedule was to operate with the Philippine Navy. We tied up at the Naval Base Subic Bay. I went to Manila on our first weekend in Subic and visited two lady friends introduced to me by their brothers. The first one was from Manila and was the sister of one of my former classmate in pre-med at Manila Central University. I wrote to her several times and promised her that I would try to meet with her the first opportunity. I accepted a lunch invitation with the family but I enjoyed talking to my former classmate more than my conversation with her. I did not bother getting in touch with her again. The following day, I visited my ex-shipmate's sister in Marikina. Her name was Alma and again she was pretty and very hospitable but I did not feel anything else. I did not have any more desire to get in touch with her again and so I made my plans to find out about Teresita Roxas in Paniqui.

Chapter 12

Our Wedding

On my next weekend liberty I decided to see Tere. I decided to just show up without letting her know that I was in the country. When she saw me, she just smiled and asked me to come in. She never had any intention of joining the nuns. She just had a picture taken in a nun's outfit. I met her parents for the first time and they were so glad to see and meet me. Tere and I were able to talk and I wanted to propose to her that evening. My problem was I did not have an engagement ring. The only things I had for her was a white purse and a gold necklace which I bought in Bangkok. Nonetheless I asked Tere if she was willing to accept me in marriage. She said yes and then I told her the truth that I did not have a ring. I am sure that that she said it was okay as I could give her the ring later. I did not remember hearing anything else except that she was willing to marry me. I stayed with the family that evening and I slept in one of the bedrooms. Her father slept in his barber chair which was just outside the room where I slept.

The following day I went to Novaliches and told my uncle Tayong of my marriage plan and that I needed their help. One of the requirements that I had to do before getting married in the Philippines was to take my fiancé to Subic so she can be interviewed and given a physical exam. I also had to file a request from the Commander of Naval Forces Philippines and ask for the Admiral's permission. I was able to do all these on a special liberty. I brought Tere to Subic with her mother and we accomplished everything in one day. Now all I had to do was wait for the permission.

I returned to my ship and now we were scheduled to operate with the Philippine Navy. We were to make a rendezvous with their ship the RPS Rajah Soliman. This was the same destroyer that we gave to the Philippine Navy in San Diego. I asked my captain, CDR George L. Skirm, who incidentally was an ex shipmate of mine (we were on the USS Tunny together), if I could take leave so I did not have to go to Kaoshong as we were scheduled to go to Taiwan after the exercise with the Philippine Navy. He suggested that I should wait for my permission as I might waste my leave because I cannot get married yet. He promised to let me go as soon as we receive the message granting me permission to get married.

We had been operating with the Philippine Navy for about three days in the Philippine Sea when we received the message granting me and Maliwanag permission to get married (Maliwanag also did the same thing with his fiancé). The exercise with Rajah Soliman was almost complete and we still had communications with them. The captain told me to ask the yeoman to get my leave papers ready and gave me the authority to ask Raja Soliman if they can give us a ride back to Manila. I called them right away. It went like this:

"Rajah Rajah this is Tigercat, over."

"Tigercat this is Rajah, over."

"Rajah this is Tigercat, request a ride for two of our personnel wishing to return to Manila. Can you accommodate? Over."

"Tigercat this is Rajah...wait one. Out."

Then just silence...

"Tigercat this is Rajah...Affirmative...request you surface and we will send our boat alongside, over."

"Rajah this is Tigercat....Wilco. Out."

The Radioman I was talking to was Petty Officer Second Class Corsame whom I met at Radioman school. He also knew it was me and so he called their captain. CDR Nadal also remembered me from San Diego as I attended a reception party for them when they arrived. We surfaced and our captain gave them permission to tie alongside us. Maliwanag and I with our sea bags got on their boat and were quickly transferred to the Rajah Soliman in the middle of the Philippine Sea very close to Taiwan.

Onboard we were served lunch which consisted of rice, sinigang soup, fried bangus (milkfish) and a San Miguel beer. Maliwanag and I were very hungry as we both forgot to eat lunch on our ship because of all the excitement.

Unfortunately, I had another problem. I was really excited and in my haste I forgot my wallet in the Radio Shack with my ID in it. I had enough pesos as I placed an empty gallon can in Control Room with a sign: "Getting married, can use your extra pesos." The can was almost full of money after three days.

I had a conversation with CDR Nadal as he arranged transportation for us. I had to go to the American embassy so I can get a temporary identification card. I was able to get one from the Naval Attaches' office where I was able to use their telephone to make a cabin reservation at Camp John Hay for our honeymoon. They had a direct link and I did not have any problem making my cabin reservation as they thought I was embassy personnel. Before this while still on the RPS Soliman, with the help of Petty Officer Damaso, I was able to communicate with my submarine. I asked them to mail my wallet as soon as possible and mail it to the Naval Attaché at the American Embassy in Manila. They were one step ahead of me as they already had it packaged and addressed and ready to be mailed as soon as they arrive at Kaohsiung, Taipei. It was already dark when I arrived in Paniqui.

Our date had been set. It would be early in the morning of Saturday, October 14, 1962. My relatives in Novaliches were also ready. They had a truck, a six- by-six that they loaded with pigs, chickens, rice and everything they needed. One of my friends, Armando Cruz was the one who would go to Madonna's Fashion School in Manila to pick up Tere's bridal gown, courtesy of Madonna, the mother of Tessie Galang, whom I met through Nancy and Brig before their wedding. I would later introduce her to my cousin, Roger Biglang-awa. They have been married for 37 years now. Also with the group would be my best man, Celedonio Collado, my Lolo Cadio, Mandong, Hernani, and a bridesmaid, Aning, and several young ladies who would help serve. My cousin, Teresita Reyes Canlas, who lives in Orlando, Florida, was one of the servers. Others were Auring Llarinas, Lina Cruz, and Minda Collado. My Tio Tayong and Tia Acang were in charge of bringing all the supplies and preparing for the trip and preparing the food.

The reception was in the backyard which was decorated with bamboo and palm leaves. My local relatives from my dad's side were also there. My grandfather, Emeterio Ramil, my cousins, Manang Mareng, Ruthie, Augosto, Patring and even Manong Arding's son, Pedro Ramil, named after his grandfather. Pedro lives with his family in Gen San where he is a pastor. He is the only one I know that followed the footsteps of his grandfather, the Reverend Pedro Ramil, who was the IEMILIF minister in

82

Novaliches. Pedro's daughter, Nathaley, now lives in Los Angeles. She grew up in Gen San and at one time was a broker in the tuna industry. She made it very big and at one point she was able to help the Pacquiao family. She is very close to the mother of the fighter, Mrs. Dionisia Pacquiao and his wife, Jinkee. Whenever they are in Los Angeles, Nathaley spends time with them. She is even part of Manny's entourage and she joins them in Las Vegas before his fights. I am still waiting for my signed boxing gloves which Nathaley promised me.

There was no guests list per se. I do not know or remember if any formal invitations were even sent out. As far as the wedding sponsors were concerned I know I personally asked them. One of whom was Col. Jose L. Bautista, Philippine Army Dental Corps, whom I met in Hawaii through friends from Paranaque, Rizal. The group all came from that town. He was there with his wife. So were two mothers of my friends from San Diego, Mrs. Poblete and the sister of a friend from Stockton, Mrs. Juana Candelaria Calimbas. The other sponsor was my uncle, Eliodoro Castro, my father's cousin. He was then Paniqui's town mayor.

I stayed at my cousin Mae Castro's house the night before the wedding, where I woke up real early and took a shower using the tabo system from their barrel full of rain water. I wore a suit tailored in Japan that I bought during my visit when I was onboard the USS Tunny. I actually had two best men. The other was Juanito Roxas, Tere's first cousin who also joined the U.S. Navy and is now retired in San Diego, California. We were the first couple to get married at Saint Rose of Lima Catholic Church at six in the morning, thus we had to do the church decorations. I believed that there were at least two other weddings that day. Considering everything, our wedding was very nice and well attended. I know I was smiling when I signed our marriage contract.

The reception was great. There were so many people and most of them I had never seen before. I know that total strangers just stopped by and helped themselves to our food. They had a feast as the Novaliches group did a very good job with the food preparation. We used the street in front of the house for our activities after the lunch reception. My wife threw out her bouquet and I tossed the garter to the group of single people. I believe that it was Alice Recto who caught the bouquet but I do not remember who caught the garter. Soon we were on our way to our honeymoon. We boarded a decorated Caretela (horse drawn carriage) in front of the house, to take us to the bus depot. The bus took us to Baguio, the summer capital of the Philippines.

We then took a taxi from the bus depot to Camp John Hay where we were shown our cabin. The clerk was expecting an American from the embassy. They were making notes and taking a survey of who were using the facilities of the camp at that time. I just happen to have made the reservation using the telephone at the embassy and I was only there because I forgot my wallet on board my submarine. A perfect example of a lemon to lemonade story.

We had a very good time getting to know each other very well. We took advantage of the daily bus trips from John Hay to the various points of interest around the city. We went to Mines View Park and Burnham Park and just like any other honeymooners we also played tourists. I was looking around as Maliwanag was supposed to be in Baguio also. They had a reservation at one of the hotels and we made a deal to get together once we arrived there. We were scheduled to get married on the same date. He in Manila and their reception was to be at Manila Hotel. Compared to us, their plan was so much more of a high society type event. Then I saw the front page of the Manila Times newspaper. An article titled: US Navy sailor jilted. It seems that his bride whom he had not known very long but only recommended by a friend of ours in San Diego did not show up on their wedding day. The guests and of course the groom waited for a long time before they realized what happened. It turned out that the night before the wedding, her old boyfriend kidnapped her at gunpoint and took her away by force. My shipmate's uncle who was a reporter for the newspaper published the story. They still had a reception, but Maliwanag returned to our ship which was at that time in Yokosuka, Japan. Tere and I proceeded to go to Manila after our honeymoon and stayed with my relatives in Novaliches. We stayed at our old house, even sleeping in my old bedroom.

We began the long process of getting a passport for her. First we had to obtain so many different clearances from almost every department. There were the Tax Clearance, Police Clearance and NBI (National Bureau of Investigation) Clearance. It is a good thing that almost always I would find someone I knew from my college days who would then recommend someone at the next department and so forth and so on. Soon we were on our way to the U.S. Embassy for her visa.

We were waiting for lunch to be over standing on Roxas Blvd., when a total stranger carrying an empty gas can started asking me questions. He wanted to know if I knew where he could get some diesel. I was so engrossed with his question that I was actually trying to figure out where the nearest gas station was, when I saw another person heading towards my wife and was about to grab her purse. Both of us saw what was happening and Tere just tucked her purse in front of her lap and assumed a crouching position and I began shouting at the top of my lungs, magnanakaw! magnanakaw! (thief, thief) I shouted over and over. That is when they decided to run. I did not bother running after them as they were not able to get anything.

We rushed to the embassy and took care of our business. We learned our lesson not to be involved with total strangers. We almost lost our money and important papers which was more valuable. Now it was my turn to return to my command. Tere was all set to travel to the United States. We also bought a one way ticket for her to San Francisco where she would be met by my family. I left her with my relatives in Novaliches. They would be the ones who would take her to the airport. I reported to Clark Air Force Base for transportation to Japan where I would join my ship and sail back to San Diego. When I saw my shipmate, he told me all about what happened and it was the same story as written by his uncle.

Chapter 13

Orders to New Construction

When we arrived in San Diego most of our crew received new orders as the USS Queenfish (AGSS-393) was going to be decommissioned soon. My orders were to report to a new submarine under construction at the Electric Boat Division, Groton, New London, Connecticut. However, I would first attend school in New Haven at a teletypewriter factory, the Mighty Mite Corporation, the manufacturer of TT-299 teletypewriter. This was a miniature machine to be installed aboard the USS TECUMSEH (SSBN-628).

Between San Diego and Connecticut, I took a leave in Livermore, California where my parents and siblings lived. Tere was already in California, arriving before Thanksgiving. We would visit friends and relatives in the area before leaving for the East Coast. We visited my Godparents in Vallejo and they were very happy to see us and to meet my new bride. My Godmother thanked me for introducing Nancy to Brigido. Now we are both married and married to Pinays (Filipinas). I brought a present for my Godparents, a new mahjong set that I bought in Japan. I started teaching everyone how to play the game. In no time everyone learned, including my new bride. The two of us became known by our friends as "Majongueras" (Mah-jong players). My Godparents would later on have a group of mahjong players playing at their place almost every week end. We like to keep our minds on the go all the time. At present, my wife and I belong to at least three groups of mahjong players.

There were three choices for traveling to Connecticut. We could fly, take the train or ride the bus. We took the bus as I still had time and we wanted to see America by land.

Our first stop was Reno, the "biggest little city in the world." We ended up in a casino where we had a one hour stop. I was lucky in one of the dollar slot machines on my first try; I got three bells and received 20 silver dollars. I quickly scooped the coins and gave them to Tere and returned to our bus.

When we arrived in New Haven there was about a foot of snow on the ground. We had to look for a place to stay as I would be there for two weeks. We checked in at a hotel downtown across from Yale University for the first night. I hadn't been paid for a while because I was on leave and we were running out of money. Once we ate at a restaurant and ended up paying using our silver dollars. In those days there was no such thing as credit or debit cards. But we made it and continued on.

Groton

When I arrived at the factory, I met several sailors like me; one of them was Frank Decaires, another Radioman who was assigned to my ship and we would be shipmates. Luckily, Frank had a car and his family was already in Groton. He was heaven-sent to us for he offered to help me look for a place to stay close to the factory. During our lunch break we looked at the yellow pages and found a motel close by that charged by the week.

Frank then went one step further and reserved an apartment in the complex where he was staying in New London, an hour and a half away. After our teletypewriter training Frank helped Tere and me move into our new apartment. Frank would be my counterpart on the Tecumseh. I was number 12 crewmember of our ship which was just a round hull about 20 feet long in a dry-dock at Electric Boat Shipyard. We had offices and bunks in a barge where we would work and study about the different systems that would eventually be installed. I soon found out that because there were really no facilities for us, we would be receiving an extra $16 per day as long as we are in the yards. This was very good news for me.

Soon we bought our first car, a used 1956 two-tone Chevrolet Bel-Air convertible. It was in the middle of winter and I had to learn how to drive in the snow. In the summer however, we would put the top down as we went crabbing in the estuaries close by which was one of our favorite pastimes. We enjoyed catching, cooking and eating blue crabs. We met new friends and soon we were part of the Filipino community in New London.

Frank bought a boat with an outboard motor. He taught me how to water ski and how to operate his boat so he would have someone with him. Our apartment was just next to the Thames River, so we were always enjoying everything it had to offer. We could cast a line from the rocks and we would catch flounder or halibut. Also, New London would play a significant role in our married life. Soon we moved into a new Navy Housing and we were the first tenants. We really enjoyed our summer there, skiing, fishing, crabbing, picnicking, gardening and partying.

As far as the boat was concerned, Frank would be in the Gold crew while I was assigned to the Blue. This would be a first time for the Navy to have two complete crews in one ship. The crew would rotate every three months and the submarine would be home-ported at the advance base. The relieving crew member would spend the first three days with his counterpart to find out the status of his area of responsibility. The off crew would then travel to the home base to be with their family. The relieving crew would prepare the ship for about three weeks before getting underway. Once underway they would go to their assigned station and the submarine would remain submerged for two months. There would be two of everyone from the Captain all the way down to the most junior personnel. Each one of us would have a counterpart.

Chapter 14

My Sons

First Son

Soon we found out that Tessie was pregnant. We were very happy because we had not really been planning on a family at that time. I always thought that I would have a son like my father.

Tessie soon celebrated her birthday, her first one in America. I planned a surprise birthday party for her at the residence of our compadre and comadre to be, in Mystic, Connecticut. We became very close to the Tibus family. The surprise party was successful. Tessie did not have any inkling that something was going on. She was picked up by one of our friends and went shopping as the rest of us gathered in the basement which we decorated. I asked Mary Celis to make sure they arrived at the precise time.

Mary Celis was one of the survivors of Charles Speck's massacre of Filipino nurses in Chicago many years before. She was the one who hid under the bed with Corazon Amurao. She is now married to a Navy man, Eddie Celis. I would be the Godfather to their first born daughter. The following families were present at Tessie's party: Mr. And Mrs. Cres Tibus, Mr. And Mrs. Tom Basa, Mr. And Mrs. Gus Reyes, Mr. And Mrs. Oliver Painter, Mr. And Mrs. Eddie Celis and Mr. And Mrs. Bernard Mamorbor.

On November 21, 1963, Tessie gave birth to Quintin R. Ramil, III.   This was the same day President John Kennedy was assassinated so the whole country was in mourning. Even the television programs were interrupted. I felt so lonely at our apartment and I was touched when they showed John John saluting his father's casket as it went by for the funeral. I could hardly wait to pick up my wife and son from the Lawrence Memorial Hospital.

We remained in New London for the next two years. Our ship after commissioning would be assigned to Pearl Harbor; but the advance base would be Apra Harbor, Guam. Our gold crew would take the ship to Guam and the blue crew would travel cross country and then fly to Ford Island, Pearl Harbor, Hawaii. I would catch my ship in Guam and make its first Polaris Missile Patrol.

Second Son

I left Tessie with my parents in Livermore, California while I went on Patrol out of Guam. I was gone for three months and Ramon was born during my absence. It was a good thing that my mother and father were there with her when she gave birth. Ramon was born on January 17, 1965 at Livermore Hospital fourteen months after our first son was born.

He was baptized at the St. Michael Catholic church in Livermore and his Godparents were Brig Tamayo, my God brother and Aurora Ramil, my cousin's wife.

After that, it wouldn't be long before the four of us would leave for Hawaii. We had an occasion to visit Brig and

Nancy at their home in Pinole where our children played together.

When we arrived in Hawaii we lived in an apartment in Waikiki. While waiting for Navy housing we stayed at a private facility and received a temporary lodging allowance, the same amount we were receiving when our ship was still under construction. We were walking distance to the famous Waikiki Beach and the International Market Place. We visited the Honolulu Zoo several times.

While living in Waikiki we met and became friends with Jimmy and Thelma Clark. Thelma used to help at her aunt's Filipino restaurant on Britannia Street which was where I first met her. She is now married to Jimmy Clark, the older brother of Lolita Rodriguez, a famous movie star in the Philippines. I am the ninong (Godfather) of one of their sons, Ed.

We finally got assigned to a house in Aiea not far from the base and I would commute to our office at Ford Island using the ferry. Sometimes I would be attending different communication schools. The second off month is used for our training. The third month is our preparation to return to our ship in Guam. I made four Polaris patrols on the Tecumseh and between my third and fourth patrol, I took my family to the Philippines and left them with my in-laws in Paniqui, Tarlac, while I was on patrol. They spent almost three months there where our sons got to know their grandpa, grandma and all their aunts and uncles. We both come from a family of seven children.

After my fourth patrol I was due for shore duty and with the help of our friend from New London, LCDR Painter, who was assigned in Washington, D.C. at this time, I received assignment to Naval Communication Station

Philippines. One of my duties as a Radioman while on patrol is to help in the well-being of my shipmates. So to do that, I published a local newspaper. I would compile the daily news around the world and type it. I invited several writers aboard for their contributions and I had guest writers including local cartoonists. One of my writers was Ristau, an Electricians Mate who was very good at writing about the daily grinds in their work area. I also had a cartoon character I called Mr. Ohm, where I drew a face in the electronic symbol. I had it in the newspaper every day. I would pass out the newspapers while the crew was having breakfast. This small act made a big difference in the morale of my shipmates.

I also personalized the family grams that the crew received from their family. They could receive a total of three messages of not more than 15 words each from their loved ones, and it was our responsibility as Radioman, to receive and distribute it. I made sure it was printed on very nice and colorful paper with a picture of Diamond Head and palm trees by the ocean.

Our teletype, the TT-299 miniature model manufactured in New Haven which I maintained, was continuously running. We receive our signals through a floating wire antenna that is attached to a reel that is housed inside the superstructure close to our sail. It remains submerged and can receive signals even if it is underwater. Our whole existence depends on this wire as we are strictly a receiving station. We are forbidden to transmit unless it is a matter of extreme urgency. Every message we receive is encoded; therefore it has to be decoded before it will make any sense.

The Navy Fleet Ballistic Missile program in the early 1960's slowly surpassed the Air Force Strategic Air

Command as the number one deterrent force of the United States. Our ship alone carried sixteen Polaris missiles capable of hitting targets thousands of miles away. It was claimed that the Polaris accuracy was so good that if your target was home plate and the missile landed on first base, something went wrong. All our missiles were pre-set; meaning each missile already knows where it is going. All it has to know is where it is at present and this is constantly being fed into the system. If we ever receive a message ordering us to fire our missiles, it had to go through several hands but it is we Radioman who would get it first. We had forty missile submarines and half were always in their designated patrol area. I am so glad we never received a message to launch.

Chapter 15

Philippine Assignment

After arriving in the Philippines we stayed in Paniqui with my in-laws and I reported to my next duty station which was located in the barrio of San Miguel, town of San Antonio, province of Zambales. I checked in and signed up for Navy housing but there was a six-months waiting period. Luckily, I found a house for rent in San Antonio owned by the Valente family located near the market place.

Mr. Valente was a town councilor and informed me that at one time Ramon Magsaysay, the ex-president, lived in the same house when he was a mechanic for the Victory bus line. It was a big two story house so I invited my brother-in-law, Antonio Roxas, who was already stationed at the base to share the house with us. This was the best duty station for me as I was now a First Class Petty Officer and I was assigned as Supervisor of Section Bravo at the Message Center.

We were responsible for transmitting messages to the fleet via broadcast. We also had a direct link to the different high commands in the area via teletype. Altogether I would have about 45 men in my section during our watch and it was our responsibility to maintain the cleanliness of our spaces as civilian janitors are off limits in our area.

The schedule for our watches were we would stand an evening watch for twelve hours, off for eight hours, back to day watch again for twelve hours, off again for eight, back to mid watch for twelve then we would be off for thirty-two hours. This was our routine the whole time I was stationed at the Message Center. There were times when I was on shore patrol duty driving a Navy pickup truck and our responsibility was to drive through town making sure that our sailors were behaving. The Officer of the Day was the representative of our Commanding Officer and as shore patrols, we work directly under him.

Once on our midwatch shift my men were holding field day, which is cleaning our floor spaces, when we felt a tremble that made our lights sway back and forth. Even our buckets of soapy water which had wheels were rolling around. We were experiencing an earthquake. The following day we found out that a big earthquake hit the Philippines and caused the death of 268 people living in the Ruby Tower in Manila.

A bad night

An incident happened during a stormy evening in our barrio when someone broke into one of our neighbors by going through an open window. One of the sons woke up and confronted the intruder who stabbed him repeatedly and killed him. Soon most of the family members came to help but the intruder tried to escape through the same window except he was not fast enough. The mother of the victim was able to strike his legs with a bolo knife as he was squeezing his way out. We found out later that we were the intended victims, two U.S. Navy families living in the area with two cars in the yard. The suspect entered the wrong house.

It is interesting to note that the policeman in our town was able to catch the suspect by watching the two drugstores in town. They followed the first person they saw buying sulfanilamide, a drug used in healing fresh wounds, which led them to where the suspect was hiding. Very good police work.

I did not waste any time. I brought a bottle of whiskey to the base housing officer who lived nearby and told him about what just happened and that I would appreciate it very much if he could speed up my waiting time for base housing. Sure enough, there was one available and I was able to be assigned to it.

We lived on Constitution Avenue right across from the Acey Duecy Club. I could ride my bicycle to work. Another good thing that happened is that I qualified to repair our crypto machines which entitled me to receive proficiency pay. I celebrated by taking a week off and took my family to Baguio to relax. We invited my brothers and sisters-in-law along and by luck we were able to get the same cabin where my wife and I spent our honeymoon.

We took advantage of the free bus tours from Camp John Hay to the different tourist places of Baguio. On board the bus I noticed a few of my men from San Miguel with their girlfriends. The first stop was a woodworking factory. There was a lady welcoming our group as we got off the bus. She would hand out a letter opener made of acacia wood to the men and an ipil-ipil lei to the ladies. When Tere and I got off, she did not even smile at us nor give us any goodies. She even backed off. This made me so angry but I held my cool. I went directly into the store and purchased a carved wooden dolphin, the insignia of submarine sailors. I did not even bargain. I paid the amount on the item then I asked if I could talk to the owner or manager. In plain and simple English I asked her why, when the American sailors got off the bus, they were greeted and given souvenirs while when my wife and I got off, the lady backed off and ignored us. And furthermore, I did not even notice any of them buying anything. This is the strongest type of discrimination I have ever encountered, including the time I spent in the United States. I demanded an apology or I would report them to the Commanding Officer and have their shop declared off limits. I even told them that some of those American sailors work for me as I am their supervisor.

She was so surprised at my accusations and quickly called her greeter who was also listening to my very loud complaint. The two of them were so apologetic and did not know what else to say or do but were very sorry for what happened. This is one thing about us Filipinos, when we meet a white person, we almost always put ourselves below them calling them sir or madam. As we were leaving, the manager handed my wife a bag full of goodies.

Chapter 16

Mario's Story

One day our Leading Chief RMCS (Radioman Chief Senior) Chase called me to his office. He told me that our command received a message from a ship in Long Beach where an RM3 (Radioman Third Class) Mario Ramil had put in a request for Duty-with-Brother and that they wanted to know if I would approve it. I said sure. I had forgotten that my brother had joined the Navy. I did not know that he was a Radioman like me.

Before long Mario showed up. He checked in at the barracks with the other Radioman on base. He was so happy to see us and also very happy that he is finally ashore. His last station was an oiler home-ported at Long Beach Naval Station. Chief Chase assigned him to Section Bravo and his supervisor was RM1 (Radioman First Class) Howard Schock, a good friend of mine.

Mario quickly got into our groove. He was assigned as overall operator but mostly on a teletype machine linked with the major commands in the Pacific Fleet. He was enjoying his liberty at the Crossroads, a small section of Barrio San Miguel, which had many bars catering to the sailors. This is where we position ourselves when I am on Shore Patrol duty.

I noticed that Mario would always be in a hurry to leave when off-time came. He could hardly wait to hit the bars when on liberty. These were the beginnings of his tardiness when he would be late for muster. In the beginning, his supervisor would just give him a mean look when he was late but soon it got worse and Mario would not show up at all. This was easily an Unauthorized Absence (UA), a clear violation of the Uniform Code of Military Justice (UCMJ). PO1 (Petty Officer First Class) Schock would not write him up and would always give him the benefit of the doubt because he was my brother.

Normally when someone is placed on report, he appears in front of the Executive Officer, called XO's Mast, and the supervisor would also be there in his dress whites and all he gets is what we call a slap on the wrist. A complete waste of time for us supervisors. Once on a pay day, Mario showed up long enough to pick up his check and took off again missing his watch altogether. That was when our Chief told me he was assigning him to my section and it was up to me to square him away or we would Court Martial him.

I gave Mario a long talk. First I told him to check out from the barracks as he will be staying at our place. He convinced Violy, our help, to move upstairs as he would stay in the maid's quarters downstairs. Second, I told him that he cannot go on liberty on his own. He would have to be with my family and me.

There were only two places we went on our 32 hours off and that is either to Paniqui or to Manila. In Manila we would always stay with my cousins the Apuan family in Makati. One of our off days was a week-end and we went to Paniqui as it was also the town's fiesta. We were just hanging around the living room when my father-in-law arrived and told us that the Queen's convertible was stuck as it was having engine problems and that the committee were frantically looking for another vehicle so they could take the

Queen home. The motorcade was over and it was starting to rain. I threw my car keys to Mario, as I did not want anyone else driving my car, a 1965 hard top, two-tone convertible Chevrolet Malibu SS.

We had purchased the Malibu in New London, Connecticut and drove cross country with Ramy in his car seat placed between Tessie and me. Once Ramy accidentally kicked the stick shift into neutral as I was overtaking a huge eighteen-wheeler. I didn't notice this but as I accelerated, nothing happened and the truck passed me as I was slowing down with my engine running hard in the neutral position. At our next stop, I transferred Ramy to the back seat. I experienced a very scary moment that I will never forget for the rest of my driving days.

Anyway, Mario backed up our car from the side of the house and pulled up alongside the queen's car. She quickly got in and Mario asked, "Where to?" She politely introduced herself and showed Mario how to get to their place. Her name is Filipina Flores, from Canaan, a barrio just outside Paniqui. She was studying nursing at the Philippine Woman's University in Manila and just spends the week-ends in Canaan. Mario was able to get her phone number and was amazed at her beauty and personality. I could tell that Mario was very interested in knowing her more.

Ligaw Intsik (Chinese Courtship)

When our off day was a regular day, we would go to Manila and if it fell on a week-end we would go to Paniqui. When we are in Makati, Pete, my cousin's son, would drive Mario to PWU (Philippine Woman's University) and they

103

would hang out with Filipina when she has time or just visit her wherever. On several occasions when we are travelling to Paniqui, we would stop at Clark Air Force Base to gas up and buy our groceries at the Commissary store or shop at the Base Exchange. Mario would always have something for the Flores family. In the Philippines, we call this "Ligaw Intsik" or Chinese style of courting.

After so many months, I sensed that Mario was getting ready to propose because Fil even consented to go to Subic Base for the interview and physical exam required by ComNavPhil before a U.S. sailor is allowed to get married. I know all about this firsthand. Filipina was staying with relatives of hers in Manila. She asked her aunt what she should do if Mario asks her to marry him. Her advice to her was to just tell him to wait until you graduate. Never marry without your diploma as you will not be successful in America. She took this to heart when Mario popped up the question she did exactly what her aunt advised her to do.

Mario was very upset and told her to forget everything. It was his intention to marry her now or never. His days in the Navy were coming to an end and he made up his mind that he will not re-enlist unless he is married. My time in the Philippines was also up and I had orders to San Diego to attend Radioman "B" School, a very important school if I wanted to make Chief. My family and I were already in San Diego when this was happening. I even left my car with Mario with a power of attorney to sell it for me.

The person who purchased our car was a Dr. Perez, owner of Sampaguita pictures. He saw a picture of our car in the newspaper with the license plate clearly visible. He liked it and had it traced. I do not know who took the picture but it was just a scenic shot that made it to a local magazine.

Soon Mario was discharged from the Navy and he joined the hippy movement in the Bay area. He let his hair grow and became a true hippy. He would travel with several of his friends and sometimes would go all the way south to Tijuana. He would stop in San Diego to see us and would leave his bag with us before going to Mexico. I even smelled traces of marijuana from his bag. My father could not figure out what happened to him. He asked me if I knew what is going on and even got to the point of blaming me for Mario's behavior since I was the last one he lived with.

Mario was leading the life of a wanderer and that was not his nature. Did he take Filipina's refusal to marry him as a failure on his part? I really do not know. My mom told me that he was getting ready to hitch hike in Europe. He will have a backpack and a round trip ticket to London with no clear itinerary. He did just that with two former classmates, both high school dropouts.

They began hitchhiking after arriving in London. While they were walking with their thumbs out asking for a ride, a black limousine stopped and they were invited in. Mario introduced himself and his friends and was telling the driver about their adventure when the dignified looking lady in the back spoke and said, "Boys, allow me to introduce myself. My name is Maria Kalaw Katigbak. I am a senator from the Philippines and on some occasions my driver and I would pick up hitch hikers like you to find out what is going on in the world. But you know what, Mario? This is the very first time we ever picked up a Filipino. What are you going to do with your life?"

Life-changing Event

Soon Mario returned to California and enrolled at Chabot College in Hayward. He majored in Political Science. His grades were very good and my father was so surprised. He could not believe the turn around. He called me and told me the good news and I was shocked myself. He graduated with honors and applied to law school at Hastings College of Law at the University of California, Berkeley.

Soon he met Judy Wong, a Chinese American from San Francisco, who was his classmate. They became very good friends and soon they found themselves living together and, after a while, they got married. A time came when Judy said that she would quit school and go to work to help Mario finish his school as they were having a hard time making ends meet.

Meanwhile Filipina graduated from nursing school and was in San Francisco staying with her sister and brother in law. She continued communicating with our mother. She learned that her sister and brother in law were going to Lake Tahoe so she asked them to drop her off at Livermore so she could visit our mother. When Filipina knocked at the door, it was Mario who opened it with Judy standing next to him. .

While they were having lunch, she asked my father if there was a way someone could drive her back to San Francisco. My father then called my younger brother, Alohalindo, who was just discharged from the Marine Corps. He was going through managers training with Lucky Supermarkets. My dad asked him if he could drive Filipina back to San Francisco. The ride was about forty five minutes long. I am sure they started talking, because two weeks later, they got married. My dad was never prouder as now he had two daughters-in-law who were former queens of his home town.

106

Mario graduated from law school and was preparing for the California Bar Exam. I know he asked me for help and I remember sending him some money for his bar review. While waiting for the results, he was invited by one of his classmates, Peter Labrador from Hawaii, who invited him to come along and they would challenge the Hawaii Bar.

Meanwhile, Antonio Ramil, whom I knew by name only as the editor in chief of the U.P. College of Law and was a bar topnotcher in the Philippines, was also challenging the Hawaii Bar. When he was checking in he was asked by the proctor which Ramil he was. That is when he discovered that there was another Ramil also taking the test.

Tony and his wife, Luz, recently visited us in San Diego and we consider ourselves cousins. Luz is related to my boyhood friend, Federico Ramirez, Jr. Tony and I were trying to trace our ancestors who hailed from Bacarra but could not find a connection as my grandfather was born in Paniqui. It was my grandfather's grandfather who was born in Bacarra. We found out that there was a time when many families migrated to Carinio, Paniqui, Tarlac when the sugar mills opened.

Anyway, it did not take very long for the results and all three of them passed. Peter and Mario were offered jobs at the Justice Department. They both were hired as Deputy Attorney Generals.

Tony opened a private practice in Maui. Mario asked Judy to now join him in Hawaii. Judy goes job hunting and found a position at the typing pool in the palace. The Governor asked the typing pool office for a temporary secretary. It seems that his personal secretary had to leave suddenly because of family emergency. Judy was sent to be the temporary secretary to the Governor of Hawaii.

A few months later, the governor asked Judy to be his permanent secretary and she and Mario became very close to Governor George Ariyoshi and his family. There was a need to appoint a new Insurance Commissioner and for whatever reason the Governor's first choice was not confirmed and so he asked Mario if he would accept an appointment. He agreed and now he is Hawaii's Insurance Commissioner.

President Marcos was a good friend of the Governor and he invited Mr. Ariyoshi to visit the Philippines. The Governor accepted and brought along with him some of his cabinet members especially the ones with Philippine background. Mario was included. President Marcos arranged a golf game with his guests and brought the Governor and Mario to Fort Ilocandia where Marcos had a new golf course. The fivesomes included the President, General Ver, his Chief of Staff, Rudy Farinas, the governor of Ilocos Norte, the Governor of Hawaii and Mario. Mr. Ariyoshi and Mario were staying at the Fort Ilocandia Hotel and Casino but there was a brown-out and of course there was no air conditioning.

Mr. Farinas invited them to stay at his house as he had stand-by generators. The following day they flew back to Manila and that evening there was a grand reception for them at Malacanang Palace. There was a long reception line. President Marcos would introduce the Governor of Hawaii and he would in turn introduce the cabinet members with him. The first person standing in the reception line was Senator Maria Kalaw Katigbak.

When it was Mario's turn to be introduced, Mario sort of whispered to the Senator that they already met. He reminded her that in the 70's she picked up three hitchhikers in London and that he was one of them. He was the Filipino hitchhiker. Mrs. Katigbak was in tears when she hugged Mario very tight. Mario was also in tears. They kept their friendship for a long time until she passed away.

Upon returning to Hawaii, Mario was asked by John Waihee for his support as he was running for Governor. Mr. Ariyoshi was termed out. John Waihee is the first Hawaiian to run for the governorship of Hawaii. Mario and John were both prosecutors in the Justice Department and they were good friends.

John's approval rating was not very good but Mario agreed to help him. Waihee was considered the dark horse in that race. Whenever Mario was invited to local Filipino events, he would always endorse his friend for Governor. On occasions when he would be the guest speaker, he never failed to mention Waihee and would ask the community for their support. Before long Waihee's popularity was increasing and gaining grounds in the election. He was elected the first Hawaiian governor of the State. Mario was the first to be asked by the new governor for his choice of a cabinet position. The Filipinos play a big part in the labor force because wherever one goes you will see a Filipino. They work at hospitals, hotels, parking lots, pineapple and sugar plantations and you name it there will be Filipinos. So Mario chose to be the Labor Secretary. He firmly believed that he could do the most for the Filipinos in this department.

He remained in this position for four years, finally resigning to join his former classmates in private law practice. They had been asking him for a long time. His salary was doubled, he had less hours working and the best of all was a membership to a country club. My sister-in-law, Judy, was never happier because Mario was a workaholic and they hardly saw each other when he was with the two governors.

There was a vacancy in the Supreme Court and John Waihee nominated at least three but for some reason they were not confirmed by the Senate Confirmation Committee. He finally asked the committee for a list of names that they would pass and Mario's name was at the top of the list. He once again called on him and asked him. When Mario told me that he was being appointed as a judge, I thought it was a municipal judge. I know a couple of Filipino municipal court judges in Los Angeles and San Diego. I did not realize that he was appointed as a Justice of the Supreme Court. The whole family was there to attend his swearing in ceremony, except for our dad who passed away on May 29, 1980.

In 1993, Mario was only the second Filipino to become Justice in the Supreme Court of Hawaii. I was so proud of my brother especially after his speech when he referred to an eleven year old boy that got off an MSTS ship after docking near Aloha Tower close to the Supreme Court building. That boy could not have known that someday he would become a Justice and have an office only block away from Aloha Tower. Only in Hawaii as the saying goes. At the reception I noticed two couples saying good bye to Mario to catch their flights. I asked him who they were and he told me that he did not have any chance to introduce them to us but if I remembered when he went to London with two friends who were high school dropouts. That was them. They are both businessmen in the East coast and both are millionaires. They read in the paper about his appointment and decided to fly down and witness the event. I wondered if when Senator Katigbak asked Mario the question, what you are going to do with your life, if his friends were also affected.

Chapter 17

My Lucky Year

After graduating from Radioman "B" school I received orders to another school which was the prestigious Instructor School. This is one school I really enjoyed going to. Going there gave me the confidence of standing in front of large audiences and making presentations or sharing knowledge with the class. Soon I became a full-fledged Navy Instructor and was assigned to Radioman "A" School at the Naval Training Center, San Diego, California. We would be in the area for a long time so we purchased our first house, an old duplex close to downtown. We paid $18,000 for our duplex (a lot of money in those days!). We rented out one unit while we lived in the other.

We only had the two boys at the time, Ram and Ray. When Tessie became pregnant again Ray was 10 years old. We ended up having two girls who were also fourteen months apart. I was so thankful to our Lord almighty for giving us two pairs. The two girls were both born at Sharp Memorial Hospital. We called them Sharp babies. This is when we decided to buy a bigger house and we found a four bedroom, two bath house in Mira Mesa, a new development north of downtown close to Naval Air Station Miramar. The house was brand new and we paid $19,000 for it using my VA so our down payment was only one dollar. We were the second Filipino family to move in Mira Mesa in December of 1969. Years later this area would become known as Manila Mesa as every fourth home is owned by a Filipino family.

After four years, the value of our house doubled and we were able to sell it for $38,000. This time we moved to Rancho Penasquitos to a two story home with five bedrooms, three baths and a big bonus room above the garage. The total square footage was 2,700 feet and we purchased it for $58,000. You can only call the real estate market in the area one thing, unbelievable. We kept our duplex during this time but soon we had to sell it because being a landlord was not my cup of tea. We became very active at our church, the Good Shepherd Catholic Church where we helped raise funds for its construction. I also became a lector and Tessie was a Eucharistic Minister. We sang in the High Noon Choir as a bass and alto respectively. Our choir members became our close friends as we were always together practicing, eating, partying and playing mah-jongg. Our children also made very close friends there.

During this time fourteen of our families formed the Pag-Asa Investment club and we purchased 82 acres in Poway. We kept this vacant land for a long time and we had visions that someday every one of us would have our own custom built home on at least two acres of land. This did not materialize as some birds listed on the Endangered Species List were found on our property and a moratorium was declared. We finally sold our property to the City of Poway for less than its market value. It was also at this time that we formed the Filipino American Association of San Diego, North County where I was the first elected President and held office for two terms. I initiated the July Fourth Committee and the recognition of our graduates. And what were the best things that happened to me during this? Well, I became a Navy Chief, was selected to attend the Navy's Associate Degree Completion Program (ADCOP) and made a Hole-in-One at a Navy sponsored golf tournament.

In 1973 I graduated from Palomar College with an Associate Degree in Pre-Law and then applied for the new Navy Legalman rating and was selected to attend Navy Justice School in Newport, Rhode Island. I became a Chief Legalman and was assigned to Naval Training Center, San Diego, California. There were a total of seven Filipino chiefs selected to the Legalman rate and six of them practiced law in the Philippines before joining the U. S. Navy.

While in Newport, I went to New York to visit my cousin, Teresita Reyes, who was living in Queens while working as a nurse. This was also the time where I found the name of Carlos Ramil in the white pages but was told that the Ambassador was out of the country. After our graduation from Justice School Tessie gave birth to our first daughter and we named her Tressy after the doll that was just on the market. Fourteen months later, Roxanne was born. It worked out for us for Ram and Ray were ten years older than the two girls.

I was playing a lot of golf and meeting many golfers in the area. Tony Zolina, my golf mentor and instructor, was one of my golfing buddies. We decided to form a Filipino Golfers Club of San Diego and we were known as *The Golfinos*. The original members were The Zolina brothers, Ed and Tony, the Zamora brothers, Tom and Fred, Gene Agustin, Cris Pascua, Andy and Ric Dizon, Nino Martinez, Joe Saludes, Cres Ramis, Frank Perez, Mike David, Mario Ressurecion, Wally Arias, Joe Tuquero, Leo Campbell, Don Lewis, Ben Salvation, Gary Hoopingardner, Rody De Jesus, Rudy Tintiangco and Mario Gamboa. Tony was elected the first president while I was elected secretary treasurer.

I also started a newsletter and named it "The Golfino Gazzette" and co-chaired our first Induction of Officers and

113

dinner and dance event with Nino Martinez. I started our Sweetheart Tournament with our wives doing the putting and we do this every Valentine's Day.

In 2003 I joined a golfing tour of the Philippines and really enjoyed playing the golf courses around Manila. The following year we were joined by my brother, Lindo, who also enjoyed the trip and he invited our brother in law, Louie Omania. We had so much fun in these golf tours that we made it an annual event. On one of our trips, our family alone made up a third of the whole group. Soon we were joined by my two sons and the two of them enjoyed the Philippines so much that they began appreciating Filipina beauties more. Today they are happily married to their Filipina wives. My wife and I spend at least one month a year in the Philippines enjoying everything it has to offer. The slogan "It's more fun in the Philippines" is really true for us.

Lemon to Lemonade

I was transferred again when we became part of the Navy Legal Service Office of San Diego and was in the Navy Claims Office San Diego at the foot of Broadway. We occupied the first floor of the Navy Supply Center. Our office was responsible for adjudicating claims against the Navy. We covered Southern California, Arizona and Nevada. Most of the claims we handled were damages caused by sonic booms and damages to household goods in transit. We had three full time lawyers, several secretaries, and five Legalman. I was the Office Manager.

One Friday afternoon, one of our secretaries, Faye Ganaden, was telling me about her problems with a rubber tree that her then husband had planted by their driveway when they first moved into their new house in Linda Vista. The tree had grown so big that its roots were ruining their driveway. She called a tree remover for a quote to cut down the tree and replace the driveway. She was told that it would cost her three thousand dollars. She did not know what to do as she did not have the money. I told her that maybe she could dig around the roots that are under the driveway and just hire someone to cut or chop it off as the roots do not really go very deep. The following Monday, Faye came in with a big smile on her face.

She could hardly wait to tell me what happened during the weekend. She said that she and her children were just sitting in the living room when a man knocked at their front door and asked her if she was willing to sell her rubber tree. He said that they would dig it out and completely replace their drive way and also pay her $1000. Well duh!!! If ever you are in downtown San Diego, go to Broadway Street and stand in front of Horton Plaza mall. You will see a tall building to your right, that is the NBC building and in front of that building is a beautiful rubber tree. That is the same rubber tree that belonged to our office secretary, Faye Ganaden. She would later marry a Navy Supply Corps Captain, William Hamill, the father of Mark Hamill who played Lucas Skywalker in the movie *Star Wars*. Bill was also one of my golfing buddies who I sponsored with Paul Cruz and Mel Gamboa into the Golfinos.

The Chiefs in our command were rotated to the different offices within our command and soon it became my turn again to rotate. This time I went to the Legal Assistance Office located by the waterfront of Naval Base San Diego. I

115

worked for one lawyer, Roger Keithley. Besides being a JAG or Navy lawyer, he was also a Submariner and a Navy pilot. When he is wearing his dress uniform, below his ribbons is a gold dolphin submarine pin and directly below it is the gold pilot wings. On his collar is the Jag corps insignia. One interesting thing about him is his dad was also in the Navy and at one time the Base Commander of Naval Air Station Sangley Point in Cavite, Philippines. Roger Keithley was born at the Naval Hospital and so his birth certificate indicates that he was born in the Philippines. He keeps this in his desk drawer and it becomes a very good conversation piece especially if he is talking to a Filipino. After his retirement, he settled in Poway, opened a law office with his wife and won a seat on the Poway School District.

One of the lawyers in our command was Anthony Principe. He married one of the lawyers in our command and was appointed later on by President Bush to be the Secretary of Veterans Affairs. He was one of the persons responsible for creating Miramar National Cemetery on Marine Corp Air Station Miramar, a memorial park developed to serve the veterans in the area.

Here at Legal Assistance is where I met the Senior Judge Advocate whose office is next to ours. I would play a lot of golf with him. Captain William Newsome, JAG, USN, was a judge at our general court martial proceedings. He was a true gentleman and a good golfer. Our Commanding Officer was Captain William Lynch, JAG, USN. Upon retirement from the Navy, he became Dean of California Western School of Law San Diego.

And now it is now time for me to retire from the Navy. I have completed nineteen years and six months of active duty, considered twenty years, and I turned 39 years old. I still have many goals ahead.

Chapter 18

Life after Retirement

We are living in Mira Mesa and our family is complete. We have two boys and two girls. Our two boys were able to experience our assignment in the Philippines so they have ideas where Tessie and I come from. Our two girls on the other hand were both born and raised in San Diego and the only move we made was to go north from Mira Mesa to Rancho Penasquitos, a distance of about three miles. My in-laws were living with us and they helped us raise our children. My wife petitioned her parents about four years before and they in turn petitioned three of their siblings. Her younger brother, Manuel, was the first to arrive. He stayed with us until he was able to join the Navy. After his training, I was able to help him get stationed in the Philippines where he met his wife, Marcy. He works for a private company that has many contracts with the Department of Defense. He volunteered to work in Afghanistan and was there for over a year. He recently returned, bought a new Harley Davidson motorcycle, and is touring Alaska and Canada with a friend. The next to arrive were her two younger sisters, Elena and Charito. They too found jobs, met and married their husbands and lived like any typical American family. The turning point in their life was the action we took when we petitioned the family.

Compared to some other families I know, my brother and sisters in law appreciated what we did for them and our families are very close. One other sibling is Conrado Roxas.

I was able to help him join the U. S. Coast Guard when I was stationed in the Philippines. I hired him as my gardener and he had to take a physical exam at the base dispensary. He passed the medical and we kept a copy of it. Then I took him with me to Sangley Point to meet my former shipmate at the recruiting office. I asked for an application and he went through the process of recruitment. My friend had told me that whenever his wife would go to the market, someone would give her a sack of money with a list of names. This would be the ones that would be sent calling cards so they can report and apply to join the Navy. There are fixers within their office ran by local Filipinos like a syndicated operation. I am so glad we did not become one of their victims.

Soon Boy would go into quarantine and be processed for travel to the United States. He was able to spend some liberty time in Cavite where he stayed with my friend from Radioman School, Mr. Tony Marquez. Tony retired from the Navy as a Chief Yeoman and settled in Cavite City with his family. During Boy's "last visit" we had a picnic at a park in the city with many of our relatives present. He married Sue, a nurse he met in the east coast. When it was time for him to retire, his wife did the same. They sold their house in Long Beach, moved to the Philippines and had a custom house built in Baguio where they settled. They were very young when they retired and they have been enjoying their life ever since.

I am now the President of Fil-Am Association of San Diego, North County. Our association is a member of COPAO, or Council of Pilipino American Organizations in which my friend, Victor Occiano was the Chairperson and I was the Secretary. My life is very fulfilling. My wife and I are also very involved with our children's activities. Our boys were in soccer and I volunteered to be the assistant coach. They were also into scouting and we became den parents.

Our girls meanwhile were also involved with sports and scouting and we sold a lot of Girl Scout Cookies. I even volunteered to be the chairperson of the Filipino food booth at the Oktoberfest, a fundraising for the Good Shepherd Catholic Church in Mira Mesa. What I did was to ask all the Filipino parishioners to make some lumpia and freeze them. I would then give a time and day when they would deliver the lumpia as it would be a three day affair. Our menu was a plate lunch consisting of fried rice, two Shanghai lumpia with sauce and a choice of either pork or beef barbeque. They could also purchase a la carte. Most of our ingredients and supplies were donated by the local merchants. We sold all our food in that three days and our booth made the most money and every one of us had a good time as our music was continuous. We really took our time decorating our booth complete with a real banana plant which I dug from our yard. I even added real bananas attached to a small trunk and cleverly placed on the top of the banana plant. It looked so real. We also had two bamboo poles and invited the crowd to dance the tinikling. We were successful in getting the crowd. Of course the aroma of our barbeque also helped.

The Lumpia-an (Where Lumpia is made)

Having experienced the success of our food booth, it was obvious to me that many people really do love lumpia so I called my close friends for a private meeting at our home to discuss the possibility of a business venture. The following couples were present: Manolo and Teresa Cruz, Colman and Luz Ebalo, Bien and Aida Pangilinan, Pabs and Gina Tejada,

Pabling and Fely Velasco and of course Jun and Tessie Ramil. I suggested lumpia manufacturing and we would hire our own in-laws to do the wrapping. We would rent a place, get FDA approval, cook the fillings at night, do the wrapping during the day, and, since I am the one that is already retired from the military, I could be the manager. It would just be a Partnership but all of us will invest equally and the six of them will be silent partners. We were able to accomplish all of this in a year. Our frozen lumpia were now available at the Navy Commissary stores in Southern California, a few 7 - Eleven stores in the area, and one grocery store in Mira Mesa. We were also able to purchase a refrigerated van and even hired a driver, my cumpadre, Rey Tagle, Gina's brother-in-law, to help me make deliveries as far north as China Lake Naval Air Station and Point Mugu Naval Air Station. Soon the Navy asked us for other Filipino food products which were very timely.

I had just met Mr. Genie Lopez, Jr. and Mr. Raul Daza. They were the owners of Mexim Foods and they wanted very much to sell their products in the commissary stores, so we formed a partnership. We would be supplying them with lumpia and pass our contract to them. Genie and Raul became very good friends of mine. Genie told me personally of his escape from prison with Sergio Osmena, Jr. during martial law which I still remember today. He invited me to San Francisco, where I met his brother-in-law, Steve. I also met Victor Lovely, Jr., one of their partners and Mr. Lorenzo Tanada, Jr. One thing they all had in common was that they were all victims of the Marcoses. I understand that there was a movie about that escape. I have not seen it yet but I am sure I would recognize the scenes.

This went on for a while but I was having a hard time because our company could not afford to pay my salary so I was selling life insurance in the evenings just to pay the bills. My two boys were teen agers now and at times I would ask their help like driving the ladies home or locking up.

It seems that our payables would just be equal to our receivables. I was very careful making sure that I pay our laborers first before anything else. I was the only one not getting paid. Soon Colman retired from the Navy and we voted him to be the next manager. Actually it was Colman and Gina who took my place. I was now free to do other things.

After a year we were forced to close down our business. It seems lumpia was not that sellable after all. I also adopted the saying, it is better to try and fail than never have tried it at all. Or something like that. Years later I was in Manila and so was my cumpadre Rey Tagle. I was on business and he was visiting his mother, when there was a bombing in Manila by the Light the Fire movement, an anti-Marcos group. Rey and I were never so scared for our lives. One person was apprehended… it was Victor Lovely, Jr.

Chapter 19

Family Reunion

In the summer of 1977 we gathered in Livermore, California to have a family reunion. All seven siblings, our cousins from Huntington Beach and our cousin from Florida attended. We all stayed at our parent's house and we utilized our backyard and the schoolyard behind our house for our activities.

Cesar, our brother, who organized the event, briefed us on how it would proceed. It seems he learned this from a friend of his who comes from a big family and they were doing this. Each married couple was a participant and must compete in all the events. Scores would then be given as to how a participant places in each event. The older kids would have a partner chosen by lots and they too would be participants.

We had many young daughters and they were the cheerleaders. The couples were Tessie and me, Carlos and Norma, Mario and Judy, Al and Fil, Lou and Gloria, Cesar and Anita, Mike was not married yet so he was an eligible partner to the older kids, Art and Aurora and Gerry and Teresita Canlas. The older kids were Ram, Ray, Dean, Norlyn, Tita and Brynette. The little girls or Liliputs were Tressy, Roxanne, Crystal, Leslie, Joy, Jennifer, Gloria, Arlene, Rachelle and Leah. Sample events were basketball throw, Scrabble, card games, a puzzle of some kind, a two-legged race and others that I no longer remember. The scores would be tallied and of course it would be announced at the awards night following the talent show. Our parents acted as judges and/or arbitrators if there was a need for it. Surprisingly it was Tessie and I who won. We all had a ball and, before we broke up, we made sure that we had an Event Coordinator and a committee in place that would take care of the next one. We all agreed that we would do this every year at different venues.

The following year was in Huntington Beach and the event coordinators were Marty and Tita. Two other cousins would join for the first time, Manang Trining and her daughter and son-in-law, Oscar and Adelita Arizabal, Preciliano and Mercedes Rubia and their sons Ramon, Joe and Gene. The committee did a wonderful job surpassing everything that we did in Livermore, the year before.

In 1979 we all went to Hawaii for this event. The Hawaii group rented a beach house at North Shore where we all stayed. Here is an excerpt from the Omania family Christmas letter. "As expected, the Hawaii Gang were super hosts providing lots of good food, plenty of laughs, beautiful sights, and a well-organized competition. Can you believe that 35 Ramils stayed in the same four-bedroom beach house for an entire week without one squabble? That is a true testament of family love."

Yes, it is hard to believe that we all lived and slept in the same house for a whole week in perfect harmony. One thing I know that helped was that we were so close to the beach that the waiting for the bathroom was minimized. If you are going to do number one just jump in the water. One event that was added was sand sculpture and we asked some people at the beach if they would judge our art work. I must say that I was so proud of our family's creativity.

While in Hawaii, our dad was able to visit relatives we last saw in 1949 and he was so happy reminiscing with them. Unfortunately this would be his last reunion as he passed away in May of 1980.

One thing that I continue to regret is that I was not able to deliver the one thing that he asked of me. He wanted me to befriend Gwen and arrange for a meeting between the two of them or better yet invite her and her family to Livermore. It was because of the promise I made to Mr. Archuleta which was that as long as he is still alive is that I would not tell Gwen that she has a different father.

The Ramil Superstars

We dedicated the 1980 Ramil Superstars in his memory and the Quintin A. Ramil perpetual trophy was established during the 4th Annual Ramil Superstars in San Diego and Mexico. It was held at Mills Park at the Naval Air Station, Miramar (now Marine Corps Air Station Miramar) and then we moved to Puerto Nuevo, Mexico, where I was able to rent a house by the beach with a park where we did the events over the week-end. Two of the participants rented a motor home and parked it near the park.

We did the presentation of awards at one of the local restaurants where we were served Baja lobsters with all the trimmings. Many tourists come to Puerto Nuevo for this delicacy. We decided to continue our reunion every four years which would coincide with the Summer Olympics as it was getting too expensive and not everyone could afford to attend. The 1984 reunion was again in Huntington Beach because the summer Olympics was being held in Los

Angeles. We skipped 1988 and 1992 because we wanted a good one for 1996 which would be planned by the former Lilliputs under the leadership of Joy and the venue was Lake Tahoe in Northern California. We were so happy staying in one cabin (that almost caught on fire). I really don't know what happened but I was told that Nick, a new addition to our family, had something to do with it. In 2000 we celebrated the new millennium in Hawaii with the Ramil family reunion hosted by the Hawaii group.

Chapter 20

East West Enterprises

We are very active at our church the Good Shepherd Catholic Church in Mira Mesa, where we are members of the High Noon Choir. Tessie was a Eucharistic Minister and I was a reader. Two Filipino priests were assigned to our church. They were Fr. Epitacio and Fr. Erasmo both from Bulacan. Fr. Epi was our fishing partner as he was also very fond of fishing. Our gang would drive all the way to El Centro at Salton Sea to fish for Corvina and Tilapia.

I continued being self-employed after turning over the operations of Lumpia-an to Colman and Gina. I continued to be an agent with Surety Life under the Long Beach Region, headed by my cousin, Artemio Ramil, who was our Regional Director. I was also licensed as a Realtor and worked with three brokers: Tess Reyes, Ed Pasimio, and Bing Minerva.

In early 1980 I became a partner with Jack Bolado, Bert De Guzman and Letty Cepe and we formed East West Enterprises. We recruited nurses from the Philippines, and helped them pass the CGFNS (Commission of Graduates of Foreign Nursing Schools) exams. They provided us information as to what books to study for their test which we used in establishing our Review Centre and found employers for them.

Jack and I went to the Philippines. We formed a partnership with friends from Manila and established an office and the review center at the V.V. Soliven building at EDSA. We gave talks at different nursing schools and encouraged the graduate nurses to enroll at our center. When we had enough reviewers, I went to Chicago and New Jersey and offered several hospitals our nurses.

Meanwhile our Review Center was getting popular. We added TOEFL to our curricula and added two ladies to our staff. Lenny Cruz Tan, who was my town mate, handled the nursing subjects and Ms. Lucy Gonzales whose husband CDR (Commander) Gil Gonzales, USN was stationed at JUSMAG (Joint United States Military Advisory Group), handled the English as a Foreign Language course. I believed that our review center was successful because we taught our students how to take the test, not learning the subjects over again. We were able to send 50 nurses to the East Coast before the demand for nurses in the United States declined. We were also exporting Philippine made products to the United States like baby dresses and embroideries.

After a couple of years we closed our company and went our separate ways. I continued my selling of insurance policies and houses. Even though we cannot consider ourselves successful in our venture, the thought that we played a part in the turning point of the lives of 50 nurses was enough for me to still smile.

While in the Philippines I was invited by my cousin, Eddie Reyes, to a fiesta in Malolos. One of his office mates was having a big celebration and almost everyone from their office was invited. We arrived rather late as we did not actually leave Manila until late in the afternoon. Eddie was then the budget officer of the Bureau of Tourism in Manila. Once he gave me and my partner Jack Bolado a tour of the Philippines as part of their campaign to observe peace and order in the country. As we were being served at the VIP table, one of the servers struck up a conversation with me after learning that I am a Balikbayan (returning resident). She proudly told me that their local priest who was born and raised in the nearby barrio is now in America and was wondering if I know of him. In my mind I know that most Filipinos' thinking is that America is so small that we Filipinos know each other. So as not to embarrass her I quickly said, oh who is he and do you know where he is at. She said that she does not really know where he is but his name is Fr. Epitacio Castro. I was the one that got the shock of my life. I not only know him, he is in fact a very good friend of mine, so I asked if she would accompany me to his house so I can meet his family. She called a tricycle right away and off we went to their barrio. I could not believe what was happening. I met Fr. Eppie's father and siblings and even saw our choir's group picture mounted on their wall. They were also surprised to meet someone like me. Monsignor Eppie is now the Pastor of St. Francis of Asisi in Meycauayan, Bulacan.

Chapter 21

Admission to the U.S. Naval Academy

Our oldest son Ramy is now a junior in high school which means we have to start thinking of college. Being a Navy veteran and having met many officers in my career that I really admired and who graduated from Annapolis, gave me the thought of why not try it for my sons. I began gathering information on the requirements. It dawned on me that when a potential candidate applies, his or her family is also scrutinized. I know that most graduates of the academy were almost always sons, grandsons, daughters or granddaughters of someone who also graduated from the institution. It was a rarity to hear someone graduate without any relatives connected with the Navy. But I was not discouraged and I became more focused with my goal. I renewed my efforts to be involved with the community and I asked my son to be an all-around student meaning get involved with other activities but continue achieving academically.

When we received the application form, I discovered that the first person who will recommend a student is the class counsellor, then the Principal, and then a member of congress from your district or one of the State Senators. I made sure that on the next open house at the high school to meet the class counsellor and the Principal. For veterans like me, I could request a Presidential nomination through the Secretary of the Navy. I was asked by my congressman to

133

get letters of endorsements from the community leaders in my neighborhood and a copy of his transcript of records from his high school.

After doing all this and you finally mail your application, it becomes one of 17,000 that will be received and screened by the admissions office. Only 1,000 will receive a letter of acceptance and only around 700 will graduate. I really consider myself truly blessed because our two boys were both accepted and both graduated. Once my oldest son was accepted, we were invited by the local Naval Academy Alumni Association for a reception. I learned about the Naval Academy Parents Club, a support group for the midshipman. The problem was the closest club was in Long Beach, where we joined, and drove there once a month. When our second son was accepted, I called some of the parents in the area and I invited them to our house for an organizational meeting. I obtained a copy of the constitution and by-laws from Long Beach and we organized our own parents club of San Diego. I was elected as the president. The vice president was a Marine still on active duty and the two of us set up our yearly agenda. I initiated a yearly event where we would gather at a local restaurant with wide screen television where we would watch the Army and Navy football game and have our breakfast. We would be complete with cheerleaders and we all dressed up for the occasion.

The other event is that we joined the local Naval Academy Alumni Association in welcoming the newly appointed future midshipman in the area and their parents. We encouraged the new parents in joining our association. One advantage of joining with us is that we have an agreement with a deli in Annapolis that delivers food to the midshipman. We used their services during special occasions like holidays or birthdays. My sons have told me that they really looked forward to those times when I would have pizzas delivered just to let them know that we were thinking of them.

Graduation!

In May of 1986 Ram graduated from Annapolis. We rented a house close to the Academy for ten days and invited relatives to join us. With us were my in-laws and my mother. About two weeks before leaving for the east coast I learned from my father-in-law that he has a cousin living near Washington D.C. that he has not seen or heard from since they were 17 years old. He is now 76 years old so you do the math. His cousin had a very interesting life story. In 1937 he was the only one from the Philippines that received an acceptance from the United States Military Academy in West Point after taking several entrance examinations with so many high school graduates. His problem was when he graduated from West Point the war broke out and he could not return to the Philippines and it took a special act of congress for him to be given a commission by the United States Army. He was also given a special assignment to establish an all Filipino company that would accompany General MacArthur when he returned to the Philippines.

They trained in San Francisco and actually landed with the General's entourage which included Carlos P. Romulo. The special company landed in the islands but they were about three days behind the Marines and so they were never involved in any meaningful battles. I must admit that I never knew or heard about an all Filipino company during World War II. Anyway he was interesting enough that I asked Ram to see if he could locate retired Col. Pedro Flor Cruz, USA in the Washington area.

Sure enough Ram found him and invited him to attend his graduation in Annapolis, Maryland not far from where he lives with his family, in Alexandria, Virginia. He is also the same age as my father in law Ramon Tiongson Roxas. The two cousins met at the parade grounds of the U.S. Naval Academy after 69 years. He invited us to their home in Alexandria where we spent several hours with him and his family. We attended most of the activities including a reception at the residence of the Superintendent. It was an unforgettable affair; we had a very gracious host and the venue was unbelievable.

When the brigade of midshipman started the parade, it was as awesome as in any of the movies I have seen. This was very real and I was probably the proudest parent there. I wanted so much to wear my uniform so I could render the first salute to my son who would be commissioned an Ensign. Ram did not buy the idea and I would have had a problem fitting into my old uniform anyway. I was in tears the whole ceremony. In May of 1988 we would do the same again. This time though we did not have to rent a house as one of Ray's classmates who lives near the school invited us to just stay with them. The Torreon family was perfect hosts. We occupied the basement which was big enough for ten people. It was just the four of us this time but the events at the Academy were the same. We met two families from the Philippines whose sons are also members of the Class of '88. They were the Abaya and Mejia family. Joseph Abaya, class of '88, is now Secretary of the Department of Transportation and Communication in the Philippines, appointed by President Ninoy Aquino.

Chapter 22

Toastmasters, Cursillo and Engaged Encounter

I was attending a middle school open house when my son's principal, Mr. Merle Fowler, asked me if I could attend a meeting at his office the following Tuesday. It was an organizational meeting as he was trying to start a Toastmasters club in the area. I had never heard of Toastmasters before but I agreed to attend.

At the meeting there was a group of Toastmasters who demonstrated to us how they conduct their meetings. Some of us were invited to take part in the demonstration which I enjoyed very much. I signed up that evening and became a chartered member of Black Mountain Toastmasters Club. Today Black Mountain Toastmasters Club is one of the most successful clubs in the district and is now located in Poway, California. Whenever I visit the Philippines I always make it a point to attend the local clubs. There are several in Manila that I have visited, one in Cebu that I particularly remember because one of its members became the International President. When he visited the national headquarters in Santa Margarita, California, which is just north of San Diego, we were there with my members and we met Mr. Johnny Uy in person. That was one moment in my life when I was so proud to be a Filipino.

Toastmasters is the kind of club that helps people like us, who speak another language, speak better English. It also taught me how to write and deliver a speech the proper way. I learned that writing a speech is like writing a letter. One must have an introduction, a body and an ending or conclusion. In the introduction is where you acknowledge the person that introduced you and also where you tell your audience what you are going to tell them. This is also where you should have an attention getter where you want the audience to listen to you. You can start with a clean joke, an interesting anecdote or a thought provoking question. You must then use a connecting phrase to go into your subject which should have at least three main topics or thoughts. In the summary is where you tell your audience what you just told them and then always end your speech with a bang. A good example is when President Kennedy ended his speech with the famous, "Ask not what your country can do for you. Ask what you can do for your country."

I recently joined Poway Black Mountain Toastmasters Club and my goal now is to earn my DTM (Distinguished Toastmaster) title. This is the same club where I was one of the founding members. Also still active members are Bob Gusky and Jack Doxey. I would love to be able to attend the International convention with my wife in Kuala Lumpur in August 2014. This will be the first Toastmasters International convenvion outside of North America.

Cursillo movement

In September of 1988 I joined the Cursillo movement of San Diego. I know that my being a cursillista changed my outlook on life for the better. The three days that we spent at La Quinta de Guadalupe in Imperial Beach will forever be a part of my life. There are really no words to describe how I felt during that particular weekend. I know I really tried my best and did all that was expected of me. There were 38 of us and our class number was also Number 38. All of us were able to convince our wives and they too became cursillistas. Class Number 39 also had 39 members. When asked why one too many, the answer is maybe someone in our class had two wives. I became very active and I accepted many leadership roles in the movement. I also became a rollista, who is someone who gives a talk to the new classes on a particular talk or subject. In one of my talks I tell the story of my brother, Mario. I was selected to be a Rector and I became the class Rector of Class number 62. Being the Rector is like being recognized and given a kind of responsibility that is unique in every way. You are the leader and every new member looks up to you the same way I looked up to our Rector when I went through.

I know that I gained many perspectives during that weekend and also touched many lives, especially the ones that I personally recruited into the movement. I would like to mention two individuals because I am particularly close to these two. They are Don Lacerna and Vic Bocaya. I also tried to improve the ways we train our rollistas. It was suggested by one of our leaders, Mr. Carlos Balmaceda, that we form a Toastmasters Club within the movement. This we did and we were joined by a new cursillista, Mr. Pat Ambrosio. The three of us founded the Fil-Am Toastmasters Club No. 9493 in June of 1993 and I was elected charter President.

Our initial members were all cursillistas and we helped them become better speakers and presenters or better rollistas. Before long we accepted non-cursillistas and our club became one the clubs in the area with the most members.

139

About ten years ago at our church at Good Shepherd in Mira Mesa, I heard a couple make a plea during mass. They were from the Engaged Encounter Community of our diocese. They needed new members and I agreed for them to come to our house so Tessie and I could learn more about their apostolate. I neglected to tell Tessie so she was surprised when this couple knocked at our door. Needless to say we agreed to be a part of their community. We attended several workshops and soon we passed the test and we were declared senior couple presenters. We hold a retreat for a newly engaged couple which is a requirement of our diocese before a couple can get married in a Catholic Church.

We wrote our own talks which is basically the story of our life. We shared with the couples our ups and downs and how we handled our own problems. My particular talk regarding our own marriage is like the one I heard from the Pastor who presided at my nephew' wedding. We attended the wedding of Jason and Rachelle Omania, my sister's son, and during the wedding ceremony I was so touched by the advice given by the pastor. He said that the secret of a successful marriage is his Five C's. They are: be a Companion, Cooperate, Commit to your vows, Communicate always and be a Comedian. This is how I start my talk on marriage because most of them want to know our secret for being married for almost fifty years.

I asked the guys what criteria they used in buying their engagement ring. Then I reminded them of the five C's of a diamond. They are: Cut, Color, Clarity, Carat and Cost. Then I tell them the five C's of a successful marriage. We were the only Filipino Senior couple in our community where our average class is either 25 couples in St. Charles or 50 couples at the Mission in Oceanside. Twenty five per cent of our class has Filipino connections and so we became a role model for them. We were involved in this ministry for more than thirteen years and attended several conventions all over the country.

In 2008 we began building a fenced-in vegetable garden at the Ramil Family retreat place in Lotus, California. This property was bought by our family several years ago. It is a four-bedroom, two-bath house on eleven acres of mostly oak trees and has a creek and an old wooden shack near it. This same creek also runs through the next town of Coloma where gold was discovered in 1849. That is why we have the tools necessary for panning gold.

This particular summer we wanted to get rid of the shack and get the place ready for the coming wedding of Ram and Analise. It would be the first time for Lotus to be used as a venue for a wedding and reception. Louie was our fearless leader as we gathered around the shack. Using a backhoe, Louie dug a hole the size of a car which we used a fire pit. We started tearing down the walls, carefully sorting out the usable lumber and burning any that was not. The good lumber we used to make vegetable plots in our new garden. I brought several kinds of seeds, mostly Filipino vegetables from San Diego and planted it to start the seedlings.

Soon I discovered that something was scratching and eating my seedlings. I was alone in the garden when I spotted a single turkey entering through the back where the fence was not yet completely installed. I got hold of my pellet rifle and knew that I had to hit it around the head otherwise the pellet would just bounce off its thick feathers. I took a good aim and slowly squeezed the trigger. At age 70 I shot my first wild turkey. I dressed it and in no time we had it roasting in the oven. Another wild animal that frequents our place are wild deer. Sometimes they spend the night under the house. We leave them alone as they stay away from our vegetables.

Chapter 23

El Camino Memorial Park

In the early 1990's, when real estate was starting to slow down, I ran into an old acquaintance, Ms. Pen Zabarte, who used to sell life insurance like I did. She told me that El Camino Mortuary and Memorial Park needed salespeople. They had hired a new sales manager, Mr. Bill Pekras, who was very good and she suggested I meet with him. I also remembered that Pen went to the same high school as my wife and she was from Anao where our grandmother was from. I also remembered our "katulong" (house maid) in the Philippines. Violy was her name. She is the same person that Mario talked into moving upstairs so he could stay in the maid's quarters which was downstairs next to the carport of the duplex we were living in. Violy also comes from Anao.

At our last weekend in the Philippines before we left for San Diego, we took Violy back to her parents and we said our good bye. Several years later I had an occasion to go to the Federal Building in downtown San Diego to pick up some forms that I needed from the Immigration and Naturalization Service. I was in the elevator when someone began calling me "KUYA" "KUYA" (title of an older person or brother). She looked like a very dignified lady wearing a green suit and for the life of me, I did not know her from Eve....that is not until she started saying I am Violy, don't you remember me? She is now living in Oceanside with her husband who retired from the Marines. They have three children and her husband owns a gas station on El Camino Real in Oceanside.

She was getting ready to petition her parents so they could join her and her family. It turned out that when she found out that we would be returning to the United States, she asked around and presented herself as an available domestic helper. She was hired right away by our neighbor. She often goes to the base movie theatre and that is where she met her future husband, a marine stationed on base. She told me that we were the ones that provided her the opportunity to become what she is today. The turning point in her life was when we agreed to hire her to help care for our two boys.

Another person from Anao is Mr. Pedro Quindara who is married to my father's cousin, Piling Apuan. My dad met them when my uncle Pedro worked for the Halili enterprises as their poultry manager. We used to order our poultry supplies from him. We became very close to them and I remember that during the Christmas holidays, my sister, Norma and I would visit them in Blumentritt where they lived. He would have us dip our hands into a huge bag full of coins. Whatever we could grab was ours. He was a very generous man and we really enjoyed visiting them. When we were stationed in San Miguel, there were occasions when they would visit us. I remember their two children swimming at the beach at our base. I recently met with their daughter, Attorney Quinnie Apuan Quindara, who is now with the Human Resources Department of the Department of Interior and Local Government (DILG). She is the legal coordinator for the Barangays (local goverment) in the Philippines.

So anyway, I met with Mr. Pekras and he asked me to help him build a sales force. I soon found out that selling funeral plans is no different than selling life insurance. You are selling a future need and the advantages are worth checking. I overcame my apprehension and soon I was selling memorial plots left and right. I already had a warm market, people who already knew and trusted me. Soon I was asked to build an all-Filipino sales group, and I was very successful at it.

I suggested to the management that we should be open to the Filipino tradition of dealing with the demise of their loved ones. A typical Filipino funeral is almost always the most expensive. There is a viewing or visitation and they also need a place to serve food during the visitation. El Camino constructed several facilities. We also started our Todos Los Santos (All Saints Day) celebration similar to the way it is being celebrated in the Philippines. We would have a Catholic priest available to bless their graves. Before long my sales group included non-Filipinos and I enjoyed helping them get their license and also training them by knowing what products we have to offer. My toastmaster training really helped me.

Chapter 24

Macadamia Nut Story

One day while at the Claims Office, our personnel officer was checking through my service records and when he saw my battery tests results, told me that I can qualify to be a member of MENSA. I never heard of it before until he told me that it is an elite organization founded in England in 1946 by Roland Berrill, a barrister and Dr. Lance Ware, a scientist and lawyer. They had the idea of forming a society of bright people, the only qualification for membership of which was a high IQ. The original aims were, as they are today, to create a society that is non-political and free from all racial or religious distinctions. The society welcomes people from every walk of life whose IQ is in the top 2% of the population, with the objective of enjoying each other's company and participating in a wide range of social and cultural activities.

Curiosity got the better of me so I went to a local club in Claremont armed with my credentials. I met the host and he was very hospitable as he showed me around. I was so impressed with his yard that I took the liberty of checking out his backyard. There were many fruit trees but the one that stood out was the one I was admiring when he arrived and began telling me about his macadamia nut tree. I know what a macadamia nut is but I have never seen a tree that is loaded with nuts. I also know that it grows in Hawaii and is one of the state's best exports in the form of chocolate covered nuts. The host also told me that Hawaii used to be the macadamia capital of the world but now it is Fallbrook, CA that holds that distinction. It seems that the macadamia thrives very well in a town which is just north of Escondido off State Highway 15 not very far from San Diego.

One day I saw some macadamia trees at our local nursery in a two gallon container selling for $15 each. I quickly loaded four in a cart and paid for them. I planted one in our front yard and three on the hill in our backyard. The one in the front yard is my pride and joy because it grew into a huge and beautiful tree that has been supplying us with nuts for the last twenty five years. It also became a very good conversation piece; whenever we have guests, they cannot help but notice the tree, especially when it is loaded with fruit.

The three trees in the back also started to bear fruit but they did not grow as big as the one in the front yard. Just recently, I gave one of the trees to my cousin, Fred Cruz, who lives in Anaheim. We dug it up, loaded it my truck and we followed them to their new house where we stayed overnight to watch the impeachment of Chief Justice Renato C. Corona.

In 2009 our cousins from L.A. came for the week-end. Roger and Tessie Biglang-awa often come and we play mah-jong. That particular week, Tessie's nephew, Dr. Oliver Florendo with his wife, also a doctor was attending a seminar at the Hilton Hotel in downtown San Diego. They also stayed at our place after checking out of their hotel. When they left we gave them some macadamia nuts. In March of 2012 the doctors invited us to their house in Los Banos, Laguna and they showed us five macadamia trees growing in their backyard planted from the seeds which we gave them three years before. The tallest tree was about six feet tall and it should start bearing fruit next year.

In 2011 I also gave some seeds to my brother-in-law, Conrado Roxas, who lives with his wife, Sue, in Baguio City. Their caretaker, Arlene, planted a seed in a paper cup and was able to grow it. It is now in a five gallon container in their front yard. That same year, Tessie's cousin, Arturo Domingo and his wife, Chit visited us in San Diego. Our tree was full of nuts and Art managed to gather some that was already on the ground. They took the nuts with them and planted them in their farm in Magdalena, Laguna. Fourteen trees are growing in one gallon containers. They should be ready for planting after another year.

Ate Glory from Baguio, a very close friend of Conrado and Sue, was also a recipient of my seeds. She was able to grow three and they are still in gallon containers. I suggested that she make one of the trees a memorial tree for her veteran husband whose VA issued marker is in her backyard. It could serve as a memorial spot in her beautiful garden. I still have some friends in the Philippines that I have to get in touch with to find out if they were successful in growing any of the seeds that I gave them. Plus, I still have to check on my friends Ben and Pearly Tangonan who live in Kawit, Cavite if they were able to plant the seeds I gave them in November.

The following friends of mine have macadamia trees growing in their backyard or their farm: Drs. Oliver and Rowe Florendo, Los Banos, Laguna; Mario and Purita Firme, Puerto Princesa, Palawan; Ben and Pearlie Tangonan, Kawit, Cavite; Eddie and Frenny Halili, Santa Rosa, Laguna; Elpidio and Aurora Pacariem, Paniqui, Tarlac; Art and Chit Domingo, San Pablo, Laguna; Nolan and Charito Ulonan, Santa Rosa, Laguna; Gloria Gutierrez and Mia Retuya, Baguio City.

Oh, and Mensa? I stayed for the meeting but personally I found it very boring and not my cup of tea.

Chapter 25

Where the Siblings are Now

I guess I will start with me. My wife and I are now retired. Tessie waited until she was 72 before she actually retired. I had several licenses issued by the State of California and the last one to expire was my Notary license. We do a lot of travelling, taking advantage of the Military Space Available Travel. I studied the system and read many books about Space "A" travel and it paid off. We visit the Philippines at least once a year and we stay at our condo in Presidio, Sucat, Muntinlupa City. We bought this condo in 2006 and it was completed in 2009. Our oldest son, Ram, lives with his wife of three years, Analise Albiso, from Bohol in Fremont. Ram works for Cepheid, a medical diagnostic equipment company in Sunnyvale. Ray is married to Angel Bondoc who is from Paranaque. He has a son from his first marriage. Shane is my only grandchild whose last name is Ramil. They reside in San Diego. Tressy is a school teacher and teaches a 4th and 5th grade combo at Clegg Elementary School in Westminster. She has three children, Maddy, Quinnie and Michael and lives in Huntington Beach. Roxanne is a stay at home mom and is presently working on her musician certificate playing the harp. She and her husband Rob also have three children, Reilly, Raegan and Reese and live in El Dorado Hills. We have seven grandchildren and six grand dogs.

Norma, who was born during World War II, is now retired after 37 years of teaching in Hawaii. She is at present on the list for substitution at seven elementary schools in the central district. It was Norma who started many of our relatives into the teaching profession. Carlos retired from the Navy and also from the banking industry. The two of them travel and stay in the Philippines at their condo in Taguig every November. It is a tradition for Carlos's family to be together on All Saints Day. They travel all over and are scheduled to visit Laos, Burma and Vietnam in September. They have three children, their oldest, Dean, is also the oldest among the seventeen grandchildren of our mother. The two daughters, Norlyn and Michelle are also teachers. Norlyn resides with her teacher/coach husband, Paul Van Nostrand, in San Diego. Michelle resides in San Jose with her teacher husband, James Wright. Carlos and Norma have the most grandchildren, eight, and their oldest grandchild, Avery Matro, is a law student at the University of Hawaii.

My brother Mario and his wife Judy live in Waipahu, Hawaii with their two sons, Jonathan and Bradley. Mario recently retired from the Supreme Court and is now a professional arbitrator.

Alohalindo or Lindo lives with his wife, Filipina, in Livermore. They have two daughters. The oldest, Crystal, works at a bank and is married to Scott Banks and lives in El Dorado Hills with their son, Tommy. Scott's father developed and owns the patent to the Universal Bar Code System that is on every piece of product or merchandise today. Scott owns part of the royalty and he enjoys his life very much taking care of his son, playing golf, and fishing. The younger daughter, Leslie Dawn, teaches 8th grade Social Studies at Mendenhall Middle School in Livermore. Lindo is semi-retired and plays a lot of golf. He continues to join the golf tour in the Philippines every year. He also owns a condo at Newport City close to Resort World. Last year he made a hole-in-one and part of his prize was a round trip ticket to the U. S.

The Ramil Retreat Place

Gloria and Louie live in Concord but spend most of their time in Lotus. They have three children: Joy is married to Jeff and has two sons and lives in El Dorado Hills. Jason is married to Rachelle and lives with their three children in Concord, and Jennifer who recently got married to Dean Clapp, a golf professional, lives in Colorado. They are the self-volunteer caretakers of the Ramil Retreat Place and are doing a wonderful job improving and maintaining the pride of the Ramil's. It has become the venue for our gatherings. We already had two family reunions and a wedding there. It is also used as a venue for the boys-only outing. Mike Doxtader is also a frequent visitor here and spends his alone time. We also have a memorial tree planted for every member of our family who has passed on. So far we continue memorializing our dad, Quintin Ramil, Sr., our cousin, Artemio R. Ramil, our niece, Brynette Ramil Gerardi, our sister-in-law, Sandy Fitzgerald Ramil and our mother, Fausta R. Ramil. The memorial tree for our mom is a cherry with pink flowers. The others are all Chinese Elms. I am going to plant a macadamia tree in a pot. This will be my own memorial tree in the garden in Lotus. I believe that the signature spot in Lotus are the Tiki Hut and Nipa hut by the pool. Thanks to Louie and his buddies, especially Bob Miller, who continue improving the place. Next is the vegetable and flower garden. The feature in the garden is the waterfall and small pond that was built by Ram as a tribute to his bride, Analise, before her arrival in America. Gloria is

153

semi-retired working as a political consultant for State Superintendent of Public Instruction, Tom Torlakson. They have five grandchildren.

Cesar lives with his wife, Anita, in Livermore. Cesar retired from teaching after 33 years. He is now teaching part time at an independent study high school in Livermore. He claims that he is presently focused on his golf game where he also plays with us in the Philippines. They have two children. Melanie works for the Insurance Commissioner of the State of California as a special assistant and lives in Sacramento. Anthony recently moved to New York after living in Hawaii for several years. He is a very good writer and continues to write about his adventures. We recently met his girlfriend, Jennifer Bautista, from Hawaii, who is also a very good writer.

Michael, the youngest of my siblings, is the CPA (Certified Public Accountant) of our family. We lost Sandy, his wife, after our family reunion in Hawaii in the year 2000. Mike works for an accounting firm and their busiest time is during the tax season. This is the reason why Mike has not joined us in our golf tours during the month of January. His son, Jason, recently graduated from high school and is a freshman in college.

Gwen Archuleta is now married to Audie. They have two chidren. Their son was at one time a member of the Junior Golf Program of San Diego. The last time I saw her and her husband was about a year ago at the Barona Resort and Casino. We exchanged pleasantries and actually hugged each other. The time before that we were invited by a common friend who celebrated their silver wedding anniversary and we found ourselves seated next to each other. It was purely coincidental. Now that our mom is now in heaven, I personally feel that it is time we meet Gwen and her family. I guess it is just going to be a matter of time when all will be okay just to acknowledge each other. I would want her to meet all of us and for her to know that her father has a very large loving family. It would be an opportunity for her to experience the love of so many blood relatives.

Chapter 26

Family Matriarch

When our dad passed away on May 29, 1980, our mother, Fausta Reyes Ramil, became the matriarch of our family. She decided to stay at our house in Livermore, California by herself. It was Cesar and Lindo, who live just a couple of miles away, who were the closest to her and as expected were the ones who visited her more often. When my family visited her after driving for more than eight hours, it really meant so much for all of us. She seems the happiest when we are with her and we never suspected that she was just putting on a show. We learned that after we left, she would cry and cry. This went on for five years before we discovered the truth. So we all decided that she should sell the house and move in with Gloria and her family in Concord. This was the best thing that happened to all of us.

She quickly adapted to the routines of the Omanias and was never happier than when playing the part of a grandmother, mother, housekeeper, cook (she was very good at this), baby sitter, fan, cheerleader, volunteer and you name it. She was involved in everything that Gloria did. Mom was Gloria's BFF (best friend forever). Louie converted their house from an "L" shape to a "U" shape using the additional spaces for mom. It also served as our venue for our slumber party whenever we visit. Our mom was always a model for all of us. She never showed any bad feelings to anyone and part of her motto in life was "Always be good to everyone, love yourself."

On December 19, 2010 we celebrated the 100th birthday of our mother. It was at the Hilton Hotel in Concord, California. Every one of the siblings with their families was present. We occupied one wing of the hotel and the event was at one of their main pavilions. We had a big poster board with our family tree complete with pictures. There was even a life-size balloon of our mother displayed in the lobby. The program included a Carinosa dance number by the siblings and of course each sibling with their respective family members put on a talent number.

My family sang Hallelujah with four of us doing a solo each. Roxanne and Rob accompanied us with their harp and guitar. This was followed by the Hawaii gang doing a Hawaiian dance. Then Louie and Arden did their duet to the delight of the audience. The Huntington Beach Boys did a song and dance number wearing Filipino flag attire. The great grandchildren also had several musical numbers with many of our cousins who formed a choir and sang several Filipino renditions. I did a version of the old TV show, This Is Your Life. I narrated her life story and called several people in the audience who played a part in the past events to come to the stage.

My mom was working as a seamstress at a haberdashery store owned by a relative, Mr. Zacahrias Biglang-awa when she met our dad. The owner of that shop has a son and daughter living in California. The daughter, Precy Orbeta, is my cumadre as I am the Godfather of their daughter, Liz, who lives in San Diego. The son, Eleazer, is my boyhood friend and lives with his wife, Lally, in Fremont, California, near the house of Ram and Analise. That is why we meet them every now and then. I called Eleazer and his family to the stage as I was telling the story of where my mom and dad met 66 years before. It was almost like the way Ralph Edwards did it.

Our DJ was Jay Castro; his father Juvenal Castro did a Lawrence Welk number with an accordion that thrilled us all. It was a celebration of her life that was carefully planned by our sister, Gloria Omania. Gloria sometimes amazes me as she is so good at what she does and of course her protégé, Melanie Ramil is the upcoming event planner. When it comes to planning an event, leave it to those two. After the talent show, it was the public dance and of course the dance floor was always full.

This was followed by acknowledgements from Gloria and me and a short remark by State Senator Tom Torlakson who was accompanied by his wife, Mae Cendana Torlakson. Tom was always considered by our mom as her own son especially during the campaign seasons as she was always a volunteer for him. She actually campaigned for Tom at Filipino gatherings by giving talks in Tagalog. It was she who would introduce Tom to the Filipinos in the crowd.

That night mom refused to go to bed and stayed on until after the party concluded. She was so happy seeing so many friends in the crowd. I am sure she was so delighted because many friends and relatives from Novaliches were present. Among those were Fred and Hilda Ramirez, Eleazer and Lally Biglang-awa Soriano, Arcadio and Charito Reyes. Also present were Brig and Nancy Tamayo, Roger and Tessie Biglang-awa, Tony and Gwen Tamayo, whose family was with us in Novaliches during the war.

A final trip to the Philippines

In January of the following year, our mom wanted to come with us to the Philippines. She wanted to see her hometown and also some of her relatives. Gloria had to get permission from her doctor. The doctor said she could go but she had to stay in the hotel. We were booked at the Dusit Thani in Makati and our cousins found a caretaker for her as most of us were in a golf tournament. Most of our relatives came and visited her at the hotel.

One Sunday we were able to take her to Novaliches to her old church to attend the service. She was also able to visit the Reyes family mausoleum at Holy Cross Memorial Park in San Bartolome where her father, mother, brother and sister-in- law were laid to rest.

The final chapter of a great life

In September of 2011 all of us siblings were called by our sister, Gloria, to come to Lotus as mom was getting sickly and asking for us. Most of us stayed in Lotus the whole week but others had to return home. Suddenly, however, we were again informed by Gloria to come back. My wife and I were landing at Oakland airport when we were informed by our son, Ram that my mother passed away peacefully. I was able to hold her as soon as I got to Concord. She was still warm and I talked to the funeral people and asked them to wait a couple more hours before they picked her up. It was around 4:00 pm on September 16, 2011 when she passed away.

Gloria found several boxes containing her diaries; her first entry was in 1956 when we left the Philippines. She continued over the years to make daily entries and now

Melanie has created a blog of her diaries and it is available through the internet. The funeral was in Livermore where our father is laid to rest. The Ashbury Methodist church allowed us to use their facilities for the reception after the funeral. The service was held at the main chapel. Her grandsons were the pall bearers and she was laid to rest next to our dad. Her marker was made of bronze identical to our dad's VA issued military marker and it was placed on a granite base with a flower vase in the middle. There were so many people who attended the funeral service and the reception venue was perfect. The planning was very well organized. Reverend George Cruz, whose father was also an IEMILIF minister and a good friend of our family, conducted the service and did an excellent job. The date of our mom's funeral was the same date as when we celebrate the town fiesta of Novaliches, September 23. Her obituary, written by Melanie and Anthony, appeared in newspapers in the Bay area and in San Diego. This obituary will conclude *Father and Son, USN Retired* as it is a fitting memorialization of our grand matriarch, Fausta Reyes Ramil.

161

Epilogue

My childhood began as WWII broke out and we became victims of the Japanese Imperial Army. I became a boy who began life doing a man's job. I helped provide food by catching fish, shrimp, and edible roots and I gathered firewood and fetched water from the well. The first turning point in my life occurred during the liberation when my father returned and I joined him in his new station in Hawaii.

Two years later he retired and we returned to the Philippines where he studied law and started various family businesses. The second turning point was when he decided that we would emigrate to America. He sold everything we owned and we began a new life in California.

I too joined the Navy as a necessity; that is, I had to contribute to the upkeep of our family. While in the service I got married and started my own family. That was the third turning point in my life. My wife and I successfully raised four children and we saw them raise their own. Our two sons applied and got accepted to, and graduated from, the U.S. Naval Academy. Our two daughters graduated from the California State University system; one from Cal State Long Beach and the other from Cal State Sacramento. The fourth turning point was when my wife and I both retired and we began travelling and became more involved with our church as choir members, Eucharistic Ministers and readers. We are experiencing the joy of becoming grandparents. As the oldest in my family and my wife in hers, we felt that we automatically became role models for our respective siblings; hence we had to stay together as a family. On October 14, 2012, we celebrated our golden wedding anniversary.

Courtesy of our children, this included a trip to the Holy Land.

We have seven grandchildren. The oldest is a freshman and is a member of her school's golf team. The second oldest is also a freshmen in high school and is involved in choir and excells academicaly. The third is in middle school and is the student body president of her school. So looking back I can honestly say that somebody up there likes me. I have no complaints. We do a lot of travelling and visiting the world. We sometimes travel via the Military Space A system courtesy of Uncle Sam.

One of the great lessons I have learned, is that life is full of choices. When there is an obstacle that can make or break us, we can be bitter or better. Be the victor or the victim. We can give up, give in, or give it all we got. I may not have made all the right choices, but as for me, I am a very happy camper.

Photos

Emeterio Ramil, paternal grandfather (See Prologue)

Maternal grandparents Rev Arcadio Reyes and Mrs. Gregoria Reyes. (See Prologue)

Quintin Ramil Sr. , Quint's father

Wedding photo of Quint's parent (See Prologue)

166

Early Family photo (See Prologue)

"Then 1945 came and the end of the war. We couldn't find your Dad's name in the list of survivors but I always knew he was alive. Your Dad surprised us coming home."

Quint's Dad Navy photo (See Chapter 1)

Off to Maui (See Chapter 4)

Parent's Years in Hawaii (See Chapter 4)

Catching the garter during a wedding (See Chapter 6)

Crew of the USS Tunny (See Chapter 9)

On Board USS Tecumseh (See Chapter 9)

This is in front of our home in Stockton with Rico Ramirez, my Godbrother.

At home in Stockton, California (See Chapter 9)

Brigido Tamayo, Sr., was Dad's shipmate in the Navy. They were very close. He was Kuya's "Ninong."

The Tamayo Family

Mr. and Mrs. Tamayo sponsored us when we immigrated to the United States. We (8 of us) stayed with them for six months in 1956 in their three-bedroom, one-bath home in Vallejo. Can you imagine that?

War picture (See Chapter 9)

Miriam before touring Quint's sub (See Chapter 10)

Miriam in the Mutiny of the Bounty (See Chapter 10)

Miriam as a dancer (See Chapter 10)

The Procop family (See Chapter 10)

On our way to Tahiti (See Chapter 10)

173

Livermore

Mom and Dad purchased the Livermore home in 1963 at a cost of $14,000. Mario, Lindo, Gloria, and Cesar attended the schools there -- Marilyn Avenue Elementary School located right behind our house, Junction Ave. Middle School, Livermore High School and Granada High School. Mom and Dad were active with the Filipino American Assn. and Asbury Methodist Church

Parents at Livermore (See Chapter 11)

Quint and Teresita Ramil (See Chapter 12)

Wedding October 1962 (See Chapter 12)

Part of the Royal Court (See Chapter 13)

175

Wedding photo (See Chapter 12)

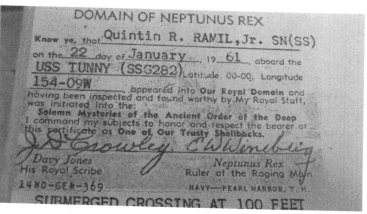

DOMAIN OF NEPTUNUS REX

Know ye, that Quintin R. RAMIL, Jr. SN(SS)

on the 22 day of January, 19 61, aboard the
USS TUNNY (SSG282) Latitude 00-00, Longitude
154-09W, appeared into Our Royal Domain and
having been inspected and found worthy by My Royal Staff,
was initiated into the:
Solemn Mysteries of the Ancient Order of the Deep
I command my subjects to honor and respect the bearer of
this certificate as One of Our Trusty Shellbacks.

Davy Jones
His Royal Scribe.

Neptunus Rex
Ruler of the Raging Main.

14ND-GEA-369   NAVY——PEARL HARBOR, T. H.

SUBMERGED CROSSING AT 100 FEET

Shellback card signed (See Chapter 13)

Shellback initiation (See Chapter 13)

Turney underway with me at Port Lookout (See Chapter 13)

USS Tecumseh (See Chapter 13)

Topside at Pearl Harbor (See Chapter 13)

Quint's brother Mario Ramil (extreme right) as Justice of the Supreme Court of Hawaii (See Chapter 16)

WHAT NEXT? "It's my year," claims Radioman First Class Quintin Ramil, Jr., Service School Command Radioman School Instructor. Must be, for he has made chief, a hole-in-one and ADCOP so far and it's only May.

Lucky Year (See Chapter 17)

With the family (See Chapter 19)

Quint's mother on her 100th birthday (See Chapter 26)

Ramil's clan taken on its matriarch's 100th birthday anniversary celebration (See Chapter 26)

Quint's family taken during the parent's golden wedding anniversary celebration (See Chapter 12)

The young Quint with his mother (See Chapter 8)

Quint's Golden Wedding Anniversary Dance with his wife (See Chapter 12)

Quint with friend Nolan, Charito and then Presidential candidate Benigno Simeon Aquino, Jr. Taken during a chance meeting at the Luisita Golf Course at Hacienda Luisita owned by the Cojuangco- Aquino family.

Quint's Macadamia Nut Tree (See Chapter 24)

The Ramil siblings (See Chapter 25)

Quint's mother's seventeen grandchildren (See Chapter 26)

185

FAUSTA REYES RAMIL

Fausta Reyes Ramil, a Filipino native and proud American citizen, died in her home, surrounded by loved ones in Concord, Calif. on Friday, September 16, 2011, at 100 years young. She was the beloved matriarch of a large and loving family.

The future Mrs. Ramil was born Fausta Matoc Reyes to Reverend Arcadio Reyes and Gregoria Matoc in Novaliches, Philippines, on December 19, 1910. Her father was a Methodist minister who traveled to various congregations throughout the island of Luzon. Her mother was a devout member of the IEMELIF Church (Evangelical Methodist Church of the Philippine Islands). In one of the many journals she kept, Fausta writes that her parents taught her to "Be always good to everybody, love yourself" in order to succeed in life, advice she dutifully passed on to the next generations.

In 1923, she met her "love forever", Quintin A. Ramil. After a six year engagement – during which time they forged their relationship through love letters that spanned the thousands of miles separating them – Fausta and Quintin married on December 2, 1934. In 1956, they immigrated to the United States with their six children (a seventh would later be born in the US) and settled in Stockton, and later Livermore, Calif., to find a "job, good luck and fortune."

A devoted wife and mother, Fausta dedicated herself to the happiness and well-being of her family. She and her husband were active in the Filipino American community in Livermore – notably, as a founding family of the Livermore Fil-Am Organization – and stressed to their children the importance of education. They were active members of the Asbury Methodist Church in Livermore.

After the passing of her husband in 1980, she became the family matriarch and enjoyed watching her family of seven children grow to include their spouses, 17 grandchildren and 23 great-grandchildren. With great joy, she attended countless weddings, baptisms, graduations, cheerleading competitions, tennis matches, and soccer, wrestling, football and – her favorite – baseball games.

It is an understatement to say that she loved life and seized every second of it. Her journals alone – which document every detail of everyday, from what she ate to what time she went to bed – are a testament to her full embrace of life and the appreciation she had for every moment, small or large.

She started each day with a hot chocolate, indulged her sweet tooth with Kit Kats and vanilla ice cream, devotedly watched Dr. Schuller's service as well as the "Price is Right", and was never without a Ricola in her purse. Her cooking was unparalleled, with family favorites that are still talked about today – including her lumpia, bibo and potato salad – and she led the family in grace before every meal.

Every month, she put money away in her "Xmas club" account to save for the family's favorite holiday tradition – the handing out of her Christmas cards and money that she proudly distributed to each family member, every year. She also donated to several charities every month ($5.00 each to organizations such as the American Red Cross, AARP and Cystic Fibrosis Foundation), poured over her ballot to prepare for Election Days, and campaigned for 30 years for her friend and favorite politician, State Superintendent of Public Instruction Tom Torlakson. At the age of 100, it was known that she would still powder her nose and apply lipstick, and would not leave the house without her heels and jewelry. She embodied grace, dignity and beauty, both inside and out.

She was never without a smile on her face, laughed wholeheartedly – even at herself – everyday, and often exclaimed with delight, "I'm so happy!" She will be missed by everyone that knew her, and especially by those who knew her as Mom, Inay, Grandma and Lola.

Fausta was preceded in death by her husband, Quintin A. Ramil. She is survived by five sons: Quintin Ramil, Jr., (Teresita Roxas) of San Diego; Mario Ramil (Judy Wong), of Waipahu, Hawaii; Lindo Ramil (Filipina Flores) of Livermore; Cesar Ramil (Anita Vanderlipe) of Livermore; and Michael Ramil (the late Sandy Fitzgerald) of Pleasanton; and two daughters: Norma Matro (Carlos Matro) of Aiea, Hawaii, and Gloria Ramil Omania (Louis Omania) of Concord.

(Lovingly written by Melanie Ramil and Anthony Ramil)

Obituary of Quint's mother written by her grandchildren (See Chapter 26)

Made in the USA
Charleston, SC
03 July 2014